British Theatre

Theatre
in the
1950s

British Theatre

in the 1950s

Edited by
Dominic Shellard

Sheffield
Academic Press

Published by Sheffield Academic Press Ltd
Mansion House
19 Kingfield Road
Sheffield S11 9AS
England

Printed on acid-free paper in Great Britain
The Cromwell Press
Trowbridge, Wiltshire

British Library Cataloguing in Publication Data

A catalogue record for this book is available
from the British Library

ISBN 1-84127-048-2

Table of Contents

Acknowledgments

The following people have been invaluable in the preparation of this book: Colin Wight, Events Officer at the British Library, who helped organize the conference 'British Theatre in the 1950s'; my collaborator at the British Library, Sally Brown, Senior Curator, Department of Manuscripts; Vanessa Toulmin, Curator, National Fairground Archive, who transcribed the interview with Harold Pinter; Harold Pinter, for permission to print the transcript; Professor Philip Davies, Humanities Research Institute, University of Sheffield; and my editor at Sheffield Academic Press, Rebecca Cullen.

Notes on Contributors

Glenda Leeming is a part-time lecturer and critic.

Dominic Shellard is Head of Drama at the University of Sheffield.

Steve Nicholson is the Head of Theatre Studies at the University of Huddersfield.

Christopher Innes is a Distinguished Research Professor at the University of York, Ontario.

Ian Smith is a lecturer in Film at the University of Oxford.

Harold Pinter is an actor and playwright.

Danny Castle is completing a PhD on the career of Kenneth Tynan and is the researcher for the official biography of Laurence Olivier.

John Bull is the Professor of Film and Drama at the University of Reading.

Fiona Kavanagh Fearon is a lecturer in Drama at Dundalk College.

Kathyrn Johnson is the Curator of Drama at the British Library.

Introduction

How 'Angry' a decade was the 1950s? Even the briefest survey of events between the Labour Government of Clement Attlee and the Conservative one of Harold Macmillan illustrates how difficult it is to characterize the immediate postwar years by easy slogans. It is no longer acceptable to categorize the late 1940s as years of austerity that were automatically followed by years of affluence in the 1950s. Long-standing perceptions of this period that have been unchallenged for decades urgently need interrogating and this is no more apparent than in the realm of British theatre, which we have been endlessly told (ever since the publication of John Russell Taylor's book, *Anger and After* [1961]) was born at the Royal Court on 8 May 1956 with the premiere of John Osborne's *Look Back in Anger*. This collection of essays, arising from the inaugural conference at the new British Library—'British Theatre in the 1950s'—seeks to begin the process of reassessment and help rewrite the conventional accounts of the history of postwar British theatre.

In November 1947, the new Chancellor of the Exchequer—the ascetic teetotaller, Sir Stafford Cripps—denounced the popularity of the longer skirts inspired by Christian Dior's 'new look'. His objection was based on utilitarian principles, since longer skirts meant increased consumption of textiles, and this attitude seemed to be the very embodiment of the dour altruism that had been so necessary during the war years. Yet these very virtues of thrift, improvization and self-discipline (which appeared increasingly life-denying) were to lead to the staging of an impressive Olympic Games in London in 1948, not to mention the steady nurturing of the welfare state—the creation of which was one of the finest achievements of any British administration.

A similar paradox was apparent in economic affairs at the end of the 1940s. During 1949 the balance of payments began to deteriorate sharply and such was the economic downturn that the government was forced to announce on 18 September a devaluation of the pound from $4.03 to $2.80. This drastic diminution of the purchasing power of its currency was extremely painful for a country that was struggling to maintain its status as a world power, and it certainly diminished Britain's status abroad, but the subsequent economic effects were highly beneficial. By the following year the balance of payments had returned to the black, the economy quickly picked up and the combination of a policy of strict control of government spending and high taxation levels laid the foundations for the consumer boom that was to follow in the 1950s.

In other words, a simple assessment of Britain's condition at the end of the 1940s must necessarily mention drabness, austerity, shortages and rationing, but must equally point to the emphasis on public provision, an improving economy (remarkable in the circumstances), almost guaranteed full employment, an accelerating house-building programme and dramatic strides towards the elimination of much-feared diseases.

This bifocal picture was mirrored in the 1950 General Election. The members of Attlee's administration were tired and ageing, but in spite of this Labour secured 46.1 per cent of the vote against 43.5 per cent for the Conservatives. However, the nation was beginning to split along class lines. Traditional working class supporters of the Labour Party turned out to vote in vast numbers in the industrial heartlands, whereas middle-class voters in London and the South East deserted the party for the Conservatives and signalled a retreat from wartime collectivism towards consumerism and greater individuality. As the cultural historian, Kenneth O. Morgan points out 'An official cult of sexual and cultural puritanism conflicted with the emergent consumer culture, impatience, or plain boredom of young people with a drab welfarized society, and an urge to create a land fit for consumers to shop in'.[1] In many ways the country was changing—the first Jamaican immigrants arrived in 1948 and teenagers were recognized as an entity in 1950—but the Festival of Britain in 1951, with its celebration of past cultural achievements alongside (admittedly minimal) futuristic designs, emphasized (in another paradox) how reluctant the nation would be to divest itself of anachronistic traditions and attitudes.

The election of Winston Churchill at the age of 77 as the new Prime Minister in 1951 clearly illustrated this, but what was most remarkable about the new Conservative government's policies was their emphasis on continuity. This may partly have stemmed from its small majority of 15, but it also reflected a recognition of the ingrained popularity of the great social reforms in the spheres of health, education and welfare that

1.   Kenneth O. Morgan, *The People's Peace* (Oxford: Oxford University Press, 1992), p. 96.

Attlee had been able to drive through. Consequently, there was only a selective programme of privatization (merely covering the iron and steel and the road haulage industries); out went the Conservatives' bitter hostility to the National Health Service to be replaced by an increased social budget; and an incredible 300,000 new houses were constructed throughout the country. By 1954, in spite of the Korean War, benign economic conditions produced a consumer boom, with hire purchase aiding the acquisition of televisions, refrigerators and cars, and *The Economist* was able to coin the term 'Butskellism' (after the Conservative Chancellor, R.A. Butler and his Labour counterpart, Hugh Gaitskell) to illustrate the seeming elision of the two parties' policies. Incredibly by today's standards, full employment was reached in 1955, with under 1 per cent of the workforce unemployed.

If young people need not worry about finding a job, what could people become angry about? In many respects, the apparent political consensus symbolized the frustration that some felt with a country that was complacent, docile and insular. The Cold War provided a chilling backdrop to domestic harmony; rock and roll (which was seen to arrive with Bill Haley's 'Rock Around the Clock') reminded the young of the enervating deference that they were expected to show their elders (not to mention the sexual repression that gripped the country); and the Suez crisis of November 1956 provided the final confirmation that Britain was a much diminished world power. *Look Back in Anger* was premiered in the middle of these events and, in spite of the raft of claims made about this play subsequently, it is arguable that whilst Jimmy Porter articulated many of these frustrations, the play's initial importance as far as the contemporary world was concerned was fairly minimal. *The Entertainer* was a more directly political work and the film version of *Look Back in Anger*, starring Richard Burton, had a more far-reaching effect on the country as a whole.

The true humiliation of the Suez conflict for Britain was the fact that the military campaign to subdue Colonel Nassar was not brought about through a defeat in battle, but by American financial pressure which caused a run on the pound. Quite simply, Britain could not withstand such powerful disapproval from its ally and was forced to withdraw its force from the canal. Anthony Eden chose to resign as Prime Minister (he had succeeded Churchill in 1955) on 9 January 1957, but it is a myth to state that the country was on the verge of implosion as the result of this fiasco. There was certainly much fury and distress during

November 1956 as the embarrassing retreat took place and Kenneth Morgan speaks of three weeks of anger, but intriguingly, Eden's own personal rating actually rose in the opinion polls from 40 per cent on 2 November to 53 per cent on 15 November.[2] The damage to the Conservative Party was also minimized in the short-term to the extent that the new Prime Minister, Harold Macmillan, was comfortably re-elected in October 1959 with a majority of over 100.

As with rock and roll, popular rebellion took on an extra-parliamentary dimension. By far the most important was the foundation of CND (the Campaign for Nuclear Disarmament) in 1958 and its much-publicized marches to the weapons research establishment at Aldermaston. But while this reflected continuing frustration with the insularity of the country and its growing complicity in the Cold War, it would be disingenuous to claim that this encapsulated the national mood. The insouciance of Macmillan when describing the resignation of his Chancellor, Thorneycroft, in 1958 as being no more than 'a little local difficulty' much more clearly represented the national mood of tranquillity and docility than any lazy claim made after the event of a general mood of rebellion or dissent. It had been much more a decade of New Conservatism than Anger.

It is against this background that we should see British theatrical activity of this crucial period and against which this collection of essays should be read. The book emerged from the first ever conference to be held in the new British Library at St Pancras, 'British Theatre in the 1950s' on 5 December 1997. As the day progressed it became apparent that every speaker wanted either to challenge the notion that *Look Back in Anger* 'began' postwar British theatre in 1956 or to offer evidence of equally significant events that have helped to shape not only this fascinating decade but subsequent British theatre. It was also clear that many of us wanted to dismantle the legacy that John Russell Taylor's disproportionately influential book, *Anger and After* (1961) has bequeathed to our schools and universities, believing that there was much more to this period than anger.

Therefore, Glenda Leeming takes a detailed look at the career of one of the most important and popular playwrights of the late 1940s and early 1950s, Christopher Fry; Dominic Shellard considers whether the early 1950s were really a cultural wasteland; Steve Nicholson looks at the Lord

2. Morgan, *The People's Peace*, p. 156.

Chamberlain's censorial attitude to foreign drama; Christopher Innes argues that Terence Rattigan was the quintessential voice of British theatre of this decade; Harold Pinter provides some fascinating insights into the acting of the period, as well as his own career; Danny Castle examines the legacy of the coruscating critic, Kenneth Tynan; John Bull compares the importance of *Waiting for Godot* with that of *Look Back in Anger*, Fiona Fearon Kavanagh argues that it was during this period that the National Theatre and the Royal Shakespeare Company were truly born; and Kathryn Johnson reveals what else was preoccupying the Lord Chamberlain in 1956. Many of these essays are deliberately revisionist and there are no apologies for this. It is our sincere hope that this work will stimulate new research, new teaching and new debates about this vital period for British theatre. As Kenneth Tynan argued in 1954, it is far better to be a war correspondent than a necrologist.

Chronological Table

DATE	THEATRICAL EVENTS IN THE UK	OTHER EVENTS IN THE UK	OTHER INTERNATIONAL EVENTS
1945	(*1944* Old Vic Company opens at New Theatre *Aug* **Peer Gynt**) *Jan* **Uncle Vanya** *Sept* **Henry IV Parts 1 and 2** (Richardson's Falstaff) *Oct* **Oedipus** (Olivier's Oedipus)	*Jul* General Election. Labour wins majority of 154. Clement Atlee becomes Prime Minister	*7 May* Germany surrenders *6 Aug* Atomic Bomb dropped on Hiroshima *9 Aug* Atomic Bomb dropped on Nagasaki *14 Aug* Japan surrenders, World War II ends
1946	*Apr* Brook's SMT **Love's Labour's Lost** *May* Rattigan, **The Winslow Boy** *9 Aug* Foundation of the Arts Council *Sept* **King Lear** (Olivier) *Oct* Priestley, **An Inspector Calls** First issue of **Theatre Notebook** Creation of first University Drama Department at Bristol		
1947	*Jan* Old Vic Theatre Reopens *Apr* **Oklahoma!** *11 Jul* Harold Hobson becomes Theatre Critic of *The Sunday Times* *Aug* First Edinburgh Festival		*Aug* Britain grants independence to India
1948	*Mar* Fry, **The Lady's Not for Burning** *Sept* Jean-Louis Barrault and the Comédie Française at the	*Jul* National Health Service inaugurated	*Sept to May 1949* Berlin blockade

DATE	THEATRICAL EVENTS IN THE UK	OTHER EVENTS IN THE UK	OTHER INTERNA-TIONAL EVENTS
	Edinburgh Festival *Sept* Rattigan, **The Browning Version** Foundation of the Society for Theatre Research		
1949	*Aug*, Eliot, **The Cocktail Party** *Oct* Williams, **A Streetcar Named Desire** (Vivien Leigh)		
1950	*Jan* Fry, **Venus Observ'd** *Feb* Fry, **Ring Round the Moon** *Jun* Rodgers and Hammerstein, **Carousel**	*Feb* General Election. Labour wins majority of 5	*Mar* USSR announces it possesses the atom bomb *Jun* North Korea invades South Kores
1951	*Apr* **Henry IV Part One** (Richard Burton) *Apr* Hunter, **Waters of the Moon** *May* **Antony and Cleopatra** (Olivier and Leigh) *Oct* Claudel, **Partage de Midi** (Edwige Feuillère)	*May* Festival of Britain *Jun* Burgess and Maclean defect to the USSR *Oct* General Election. Conservatives win majority of 17. Winston Churchill becomes Prime Minister	*Oct* Renewal of Korean Armistice talks
1952	*Mar*, Rattigan, **The Deep Blue Sea** *Oct* **Porgy and Bess**	*Feb* George VI dies	*Nov* General Eisenhower elected US President
1953	*May* **Guys and Dolls** *Nov* Rattigan, **The Sleeping Prince** *Dec* Hunter, **A Day by the Sea** First issue of **Plays and Players** Theatre Workshop take up the lease of the The-atre Royal, Stratford East	*Jun* Coronation of Elizabeth II	*Jun* Korean Armistice signed *Sep* Khrushchev becomes First Secretary of the Communist Party, USSR
1954	*Mar* Whiting, **Marching Song** *Sept* **Separate Tables**	*Jul* Food rationing ends	*Dec* US senate 'condemns' McCarthy 'witch-trials'

DATE	THEATRICAL EVENTS IN THE UK	OTHER EVENTS IN THE UK	OTHER INTERNA-TIONAL EVENTS
	Sept Kenneth Tynan becomes the Theatre Critic of *The Observer*		
1955	*Jan* Theatre Workshop's **Richard II** *Mar* Ionesco, **The Lesson**, (Arts) *Jul* Brecht, **Mother Courage** (Joan Littlewood) *3 Aug* Beckett, **Waiting for Godot**, (Arts) *Aug* **Titus Andronicus** (dir.Brook, Olivier)	*May* General Election. Conservatives win majority of 60. Anthony Eden becomes Prime Minister *Jul* Execution of Ruth Ellis spurs campaign to end capital punishement *Sept* Commercial TV introduced	*Jul* European Parliament holds first meeting in Strasbourg
1956	*Apr* Opening season of the English Stage Company (ESC) at the Royal Court *8 May* Osborne, **Look Back In Anger** *May* Behan, **The Quare Fellow** *Aug* Berliner Ensemble's **Mother Courage** (Helene Weigel) *Nov* ESC's **The Good Person of Setzuan** Foundation of the National Youth Theatre	*Apr* Khrushchev visits Britain	*26 Jul* Nassar nationalises the Suez Canal *30 Oct* Soviet troops invade Hungary *5 Nov* British and French troops land at Port Said; intervention aborted two days later *Nov* Re-election of President Eisenhower
1957	*Apr* Osborne, **The Entertainer** *Apr* Beckett, **Fin de Partie**	*9 Jan* Eden resigns as Prime Minister following Suez debacle, Harold Macmillan succeeds him *25 Jul* Macmillan 'Most of our people have never had it so good' *Sep* Wolfenden Report on homosexuality	*25 Mar* EEC established with the Treaty of Rome *Oct* Sputniks launched
1958	*Jan* Wesker, **Chicken Soup With Barley** *May* Pinter, **The Birthday Party**	*Feb* Campaign for Nuclear Disarmament launched	*Jan* Common Market comes into force

DATE	THEATRICAL EVENTS IN THE UK	OTHER EVENTS IN THE UK	OTHER INTERNA-TIONAL EVENTS
	Oct Behan, **The Hostage** *Nov* Delaney, **A Taste of Honey**, *Dec* **West Side Story** Belgrade Theatre, Coventry, opens Lord Chamberlain's secret memorandum on homosexuality		
1959	*Jul* Wesker, **Roots** *Oct* Arden, **Serjeant Musgrave's Dance**, Royal Court Nottingham Playhouse opens	*Feb* Macmillan visits Moscow *8 Oct* General Election. Conservatives win majority of 100.	*Jan* De Gaulle proclaimed President of the Fifth Republic

The Early 1950s: Transfers, Temptations and Turning Point in the Career of Christopher Fry (*Venus Observ'd, A Sleep of Prisoners* and *The Dark Is Light Enough*)

Glenda Leeming

In the early 1950s, Christopher Fry was one of the best known and most promising playwrights in Britain. In this paper I am going to suggest that the qualities that made him successful were closely—perhaps indeed too closely—bound up with the conditions of production and consumption of commercial theatre in the 1950s, and militated against him developing in a different direction in the 1960s and after; I am not simply saying that his plays fitted a transient theatrical mode or coincided with a particular spirit of the age, which is true of more or less any temporarily successful playwright one could mention, but rather that his theatrical skills were important to successful theatrical production, while containing seeds of vulnerability that impeded his potential development.

In some respects Fry's best known works, his comedies, epitomize late 1940s and early 1950s West End theatre output. West End comedies, thrillers and farces (and musicals) were of course not peculiar to the 1950s; similar fare is still with us today. The problem that critics like Tynan detected in the 1950s was that there seemed to be nothing else but the most anodyne and uninteresting type of comedies, thrillers and farces. Even Shaw had died in 1950. At the same time, society was felt to be changing, but the comedies and thrillers on offer were not changing, and were not taking into account new perspectives. These generalizations, which are rife in surveys of the 1950s, as in all decade surveys, belie the many complexities of social change: in the 1950s evidence is plentiful to show that, in spite of social changes, public opinion was retrospective, reactionary and wedded to tradition. But it seems fair to say that Fry was one of the dramatists of the time who was trying to do something different, and not only in the verse form of his dialogue.

Implicit in the criticism of Tynan and others is the suggestion that West End comedies in general no longer bore any relation to the classic functions of comedy, to correct manners and morals, but merely reinforced the assumptions and attitudes of its audiences. Fry however had a philosophical concern with the spiritual development of humankind, partly through its learning pacifism, tolerance and feeling for others. He therefore criticizes violence, intolerance and self-centredness. I say 'philosophical', because underlying the perennial and recognizable message of 'be nice to each other' was an adherence to the ideas of Berdyaev and Teilhard de Chardin, although allusions to the wider religio-philosophical framework is effaced to the point of invisibility in the plays. At least this criticism of personal intolerance and selfishness, and more radically, of all war, force and recourse to violence whatever the pretext, provided a coherent and well-based moral foundation for his plays. His comedies, then, correct not just manners but underlying moral attitudes, where the average West End comedy reinforced the status quo and questioned nothing.

In spite of their moral purpose, however, the comedies *The Lady's Not for Burning, Venus Observ'd*, and *The Dark Is Light Enough* were intricately involved in the West End. *The Lady's Not for Burning* (1948) was commissioned by Alec Clunes for the Arts Theatre Club, and was launched into the West End in 1949 because, when Clunes wanted to sell his rights to the play, he sent it to John Gielgud, and Gielgud told Binkie Beaumont of the H.M. Tennent management that he 'must get it' for him.[1] Olivier's commissioning of *Venus Observed* followed, and Edith Evans asked for a play for herself after that. Fry was seen as a generator of star parts, and a bankable star can put on a play, or get someone else to put on a play.

This led to commercial success for Fry in the early 1950s. In 1950 alone, the production of *Venus Observ'd* was playing while his translation of Anouilh's *L'Invitation au Chateau* as *Ring Round the Moon* was being performed; a professional production of his *Boy with a Cart* was also running at the Lyric Theatre, Hammersmith, and *The Lady's Not for Burning* had only just closed late in 1949, and was about to be relaunched in New York. *Venus Observ'd* (1950) particularly seems to epitomize West End comedy of the 1950s: its hero is titled and lives in a castle with an observatory; none of the characters have any economic relationship with

---

1.   John Gielgud in collaboration with John Miller and John Powell, *An Actor and his Times* (London: Sidgwick and Jackson, 1979), p. 162.

society, in that they do not work (the steward is increasing his market level wages by embezzling the duke's money, secretly condoned and legitimated by the duke; the butler is a burglar, employed on a whim, and another manservant is a lion tamer who has lost his nerve, also employed on a whim; these are more like the characters who accompany Dorothy to Oz than part of the twentieth-century social fabric.) The heroine has indeed been imprisoned briefly for violent protest, but this was an aesthetic protest (destroying offensively ugly buildings and monuments) rather than a social, political or economic one.

Nonetheless the play has a message of its own: in classic corrective comedic manner, the duke has to learn to care for others even at the expense of sacrificing himself, and Perpetua, our heroine, has to decide to do what is right, even if it means sacrificing the father she loves. It is a perfectly acceptable traditional comedy, without relating particularly to twentieth-century circumstances.

The lesson we learn from this is that Fry was not interested in depicting 1950s England in any particular detail, in its specific and changing problems. To support this, there is Fry's experience as a dramatist outside the commercial theatre of the time. As noted above, a major preoccupation of his work is with the use of force, whether personal violence, state enforcement or organized warfare, a subject probably focused for him in the dilemma he encountered as a pacifist of how to act in the second world war. Fry was asked to write *A Sleep of Prisoners* (1951) for the Festival of Britain, and this was a play which was outside his West End framework.

Sleep was planned to tour churches, and according to his own dictum 'you write, on the whole, for what is there',[2] Fry planned it to fit a church; he recalled afterwards 'I remember feeling a pleasant freedom in writing *A Sleep of Prisoners*'.[3] In conformity with the needs of theatre economy, two of his comedies, *A Phoenix Too Frequent* and *Lady*, had had single sets, and *Venus* and *The Dark Is Light Enough* had two sets, with the necessary manipulation of pretexts for getting the characters in and out of these sets in the desired combinations. In *Sleep* the actual church in which the play was being staged supplied the framing set, that is, it becomes the church in which the characters, who are four soldier

---

2.   Christopher Fry, 'Talking of Henry', *Twentieth Century* 169 (1961), pp. 186-90 (188).

3.   Fry, 'Talking of Henry', p. 188.

prisoners-of-war, are imprisoned, and it merges into the nebulous areas where the soldiers' dreams are enacted; in the dream sequences the action is set anywhere or nowhere, or in places that change fluidly as the action progresses, with for instance the pulpit functioning sometimes as the top of a hill, sometimes as a tree. There was thus no constriction by the needs of a practicable set with so many doors and windows and lines of dialogue to explain why people had come in or gone out.

There is fluidity too in the presentation of characters, because in the four successive dream sequences, four different dreamers in turn are meant to be giving their own subjective version of their fellow prisoners—caricatured or distorted in some cases, and thus changing from episode to episode. The language is even more inventive than in the seasonal comedies, because in the dream sequences there is no imitation of conversation, but it is also more compressed, with few long explanatory speeches, which possibly is why some critics at the time thought that Fry had tamed the exuberance and inventiveness of his language (though as I say it actually goes further into distortion and innovation than before). There are occasional comic lines, but it is not a comedy. The message, though some found it confusing at the time, is as clear or clearer than Fry's most explicit comedy *Dark*: force of all kinds should be avoided, and tolerance and passive resistance should be embraced. The sin of Cain, with which the episodic dream sequences begin, must be resisted, both as the personal murderous impulse and as the more sophisticated, specious arguments for exterminating external and internal enemies.

It seems then that both in theme and staging *Sleep* showed that Fry was perfectly capable of producing plays of an experimental and unconventional kind. It is worth noting the similarities between *Sleep* and *Serjeant Musgrave's Dance*, where both plays use the 'group of soldiers in isolation' convention (the old one, the aggressive one, the jokey one etc.) for an ultimately pacifist message, with imagery of fire and apocalyptic revelation.

Arden was one of several dramatists who enjoyed and reflected on Fry's work, and it seems possible to suggest that Fry's drama was influential because it contained many elements which were acceptable and viable for the coming decade; Fry himself could have gone on to write further radical and imagistic plays.

With his next play *The Dark Is Light Enough* (1954), however, although Fry sharpened his pacifist message, he returned to the conventional comedic formula. Fry wanted to write about a moment of crisis in a revolutionary setting, and took a historical revolution, the rebellion of the Hungarians against the Austro-Hungarian Empire. The central character, the countess, is committed mainly to passive resistance and non-violent opposition (though she leaves a loophole to this) and does not sympathize with the attempt to gain freedom by armed uprising. Like Perpetua eventually withdrawing her protection from her father, the countess refuses to reprieve her captured son-in-law, taken hostage by the rebels, by revealing where she has hidden the much disliked and hunted deserter Gettner.

This is a highly effective and forceful play, and various people noted that Edith Evans had perhaps done it no service by overlaying its actual message with a layer of magnetic personal charm. It is, however, not written in the pared-down, free-wheeling style of *Sleep*, but is constructed in the characteristic way of Fry's other full length comedies, with a largish cast, a number of cameo roles and a well-wrought variety of crowd scenes and intimate dialogues, climaxes and quiet meditative moments. Big entrances, moments of reversal, ominous knocking at the door, an off-stage shot, are some of the well worn theatrical devices that Fry, perhaps piqued by criticisms that *Venus* had lacked plot and suspense, worked into *Dark*. This, I suggest, shows the attraction, the tie, the temptation of the theatrical mainstream for a writer who was good at it, against his potential for developing differently.

This strong theatrical element points to the fact that, unlike other writers of poetic drama, Fry began his adult life with a simultaneous commitment to and experience of theatre and poetry. Some dramatists had no experience at all of acting and being directed, of experiencing the play from inside, as it were, and others had perhaps one or two experiences of only one type of performance. This is different from regular participation in all kinds of work in all kinds and sizes of company, in all kinds of theatre. Fry wrote poetry like many adolescents, but went on writing it as an adult, and at the same time his first job after leaving school was in a minor provincial theatre. Throughout the late 1920s and 1930s he moved from precarious job to job in the theatre, in London and the provinces, in a hand-to-mouth existence that nonetheless familiarized him with theatre conditions and a wide range of dramatic genres. He wrote, acted, directed and was directed, all salutary experiences, and worked in London and the provinces, in amateur plays, musicals, on tour, and in weekly rep. Most poetic dramatists, indeed most dramatists, have a far less extensive experience than this. So from this point of view,

Fry had a better claim than many to be a man of the theatre, rather than a literary outsider forcing theoretic ideas on the profession.

At the same time, however, Fry's theatrical experience accustomed him to the commercial scale of values, understandably, in which a long West End run with big stars is the ultimate accolade. (Fry recalls Olivier commiserating with him that the RSC had in 1962 put on *Curtmantle* with a cast of unknowns, such as Derek Godfrey and Susan Fleetwood). The confirmation of success was transfer to the West End, not production in outlying theatres. *Lady* made Fry a household name, but only when it transferred from the Arts to the Globe. *The Firstborn* (1948) never reached its full potential, because its transfer from Edinburgh to London was unsuccessful. Similarly when *Sleep* transferred from church to theatre, critics commented that Fry was 'preaching'[4] and that this was not a theatrical play. The message of the transfer test was that certain plays were not acceptable to the mainstream of commercial theatre.

Another of Fry's virtues as a dramatist is his flexibility. It is clear from a survey of Fry's career that he is a writer who responds well to others' requirements. Up to and including *Dark*, most of his plays were requested or even commissioned by a consumer—in the 1930s he was asked to produce plays about Dr Barnardo or for the Girls Friendly Society; his first play to attract attention, *The Boy with a Cart* (1938), was requested by the local vicar for the village fete, until *Phoenix* (1946) written at Martin Browne's request for his Poetic Drama Season at the Mercury led to Alec Clunes's commission and the sequence of successes listed above. The only exceptions to this are *The Firstborn* and *Curtmantle*, which he wrote without a commission and without a deadline, and they caused him literally years of travail.

What then happened in the mid-1950s to interrupt the flow of satisfactory plays? Why did Fry not go on to write his final seasonal comedy, *A Yard of Sun* (1970), straightaway? The idea of writing about Henry II and the thirteenth century had come to him in 1950, and there were hopes that Olivier would be interested in playing Henry. But 'what with one thing and another', Fry said, he delayed starting it, and Olivier never offered him a firm deadline or a firm promise.

In the event, Fry responded to the temptations of immediate commissions which were pressing upon him throughout the 1950s. Even while working on *Dark* he wrote the script for the coronation film, *A Queen Is Crowned* (1953) and adapted Peter Brook's film of *The Beggar's Opera*

4.   Ivor Brown, *The Observer*, 12 May 1951, p. 6.

(1953). After 1954, he translated more Anouilh and began translating Giraudoux, then went to Italy and worked with film-makers on *Ben Hur* (1958). If Olivier had gone straight on to insist on *Curtmantle*, or even the summer comedy to be ready in 1956, or if the Royal Court had asked for a pacifist play about Korea, things might have turned out differently. Instead Fry kept the Henry play at the back of his mind and his desk, and gave immediate attention to the commissions that were coming in.

Apart from the incentive of positive commissions, there was also a problem of detachment from the theatrical process. This was the turning point in Fry's career. He said that for quite some time he 'went through a kind of crisis of confidence in my own ability to express the world as I saw it in terms of the modern theatre'.[5] The adaptability that enabled him to build a play around a named actor needed the stimulus of having that actor ask for a play, as well as his own inspiration.

Certainly there are some interesting things in *Curtmantle* (it takes place in William Marshall's head, there is the fog scene, the scenes move fluidly from one to another—for instance a sentence is begun in France and concluded in England) but otherwise it is a straightforward chronicle play, and therefore, being the only history play Fry wrote, lacked the flexibility and scope he had found in myth and biblical stories. It did not appear in London until 1962, and eight years is a long time in the theatre; its lack of success meant that Fry went back to more translations, films and television adaptations.

Fry's familiarity with the theatre and his flexibility as a writer then tended to work against him in the changing world of 1950s drama. It is not, of course, a bad thing to be professional as a dramatist, to know what can be done on stage, or to produce different types of plays for different situations; but these are virtues which in Fry needed triggering by the given theatrical circumstances. As the Religious Drama movement lost influence on him, and there was no way in which he was involved in new theatrical ventures (by the late 1950s he was 50 years old, not a 'new writer' to be encouraged by Royal Court writers groups), stimuli from the world of theatre dried up. It would still have been possible for Fry to write in new styles after 1954—he was after all flexible—but possibly because he was identified with the old regime against which directors and theatre groups were reacting, no stimulus from the more experimental areas of theatre was forthcoming.

5.   Fry, 'Talking of Henry', p. 186.

As noted above, the reaction against his plays is usually related to the revival of realism in the so called New Wave of British Drama, and the advent of Absurdist drama from Europe. But how far did this actually affect the West End? Light comedies, farces, thrillers and revivals of the classics continued virtually as usual, as they do today. Was the audience for Fry's plays a particular subsection which craved novelty and turned from poetic drama to kitchen sink? It seems unlikely that audience behaviour was as clearcut as this. Harold Hobson had written of *The Lady's Not for Burning:*

> It pleased every kind of playgoer. Charwomen liked it. Members of the peerage liked it; elderly maiden ladies and undergraduates liked it, and so did intellectuals. I took a box during the Christmas holidays for my schoolgirl daughter, aged 13. She liked it enormously, and so far as we could judge, so did Princess Margaret, whom we could see quite plainly in the front row of the stalls. The play paid off its production expenses in seven weeks, and then ran at a profit for another thirty.[6]

These are the audiences who go to see a star performer in an entertaining comedy, and would continue to do so, regardless of changing theatrical trends elsewhere.

In conclusion, I have no answer as to why no further dominant West End stars or managements demanded plays from him. Rather than campaign to reassert himself, Fry took the offers of the film and television industry, and wrote translations, film scripts and adaptations. The interaction of the conditions of West End theatre, and of the commercial entertainment business in general, its mindset and commercial rewards, made a paralysing combination with Fry's own qualities of professional expertise and responsiveness to circumstances.

6.   Harold Hobson, *New York Times*, section VI, 12 March 1950, p. 24. The same points are made by E. Martin Browne in 'From T.S. Eliot to Christopher Fry', *Adam* 19 (1951), pp. 14-16 (16).

1950–54: Was it a Cultural Wasteland?

Dominic Shellard

While I was at school my English teacher was convinced that postwar British theatre had begun on 8 May 1956, when the curtain rose on the stage of the Royal Court to reveal Alison Porter ironing in *Look Back in Anger*. It has proved an enduring fallacy. This essay was conceived to interrogate the notion that the 'big bang' of theatrical creativity centred around the English Stage Company in 1956 was the only event in the reorientation of British drama. Before I proceed to do this, however, I wish to cite some first-hand testimony about three milestone plays of this decade—*Waiting for Godot* (1955), *Look Back in Anger* (1956) and *A Taste of Honey* (1958)—as evidence of the value of looking afresh at this period of theatrical upheaval.

As part of my research for a book on postwar British theatre,[1] I consulted Jack Reading, the vice-president of the Society for Theatre Research. He has a clear memory and an unrivalled experience of London theatre-going since the war and is one of the very few people who was at the first night of both *Waiting for Godot* and *Look Back in Anger* and who witnessed *A Taste of Honey* in its first week. His recollections are intriguing:

> *Waiting for Godot* left the members of its audience who sat it out to the end completely *stunned*. We knew we had seen things on the stage that could not be related to anything theatrical previously experienced. It was almost beyond discussion or rational appraisal. It had been an entirely new experience: a play (for want of a better word) that had taken its audience into a new extension of imagination.
>
> *Look Back in Anger*, on the other hand, was merely *stimulating*: the set had been accepted as not un-ordinary and not as ground-breaking as some

---

1. Dominic Shellard, *British Theatre Since 1945* (New Haven: Yale University Press, 1999).

later commentators now suggest; the characters, the story and the plotting were unremarkable; we knew of graduates who had declined to enter the rat-race of usual employment; the direction was pedestrian and the final curtain of animal talk had been squirmishly embarrassing. What had been different was the vehemence of the delivery of the off-the-top outbursts of Jimmy.

The point I am making is that the claim now made for the play as the water-shed of post-war theatre is something developed *after* the event. It did not seem so at the time. Its importance is a myth which, like all myths, feeds on itself, and very much aided, by that brilliant coinage of the Angry Young Man. This has given journalists and writers a caption head-line much in the same way as the later catch 'Kitchen Sink' had to explain the exploration, dramatically, of every-day working and low life.

Which brings me to the premise that *A Taste of Honey* has been over-looked as an example of a new theatre in advance of its time—and in many ways. The set was just as squalid as that for *Look Back in Anger* but nothing like as conventionally realised. John Bury was using financial re-straints to explore a new field of scenic suggestion rather than social real-ism. The story line was certainly taboo breaking, revealing a lifestyle, presumed to exist but seldom touching on the lives of most folk in the audience—a mother practically on-the-game, a pimp of a boyfriend, an unschooled neglected daughter, a coloured boy pick-up (in a scene of intense poignancy), a pregnancy (YES black-white coitus: the ultimate dread), and the homosexual help-mate (this itself a revolution on stage, permissible presumably because his homosexuality was not discussed or practised).

A Taste of Honey was being considered and gestated at about the same time as *Look Back in Anger* but reached the stage later, yet it has an equal, if not greater, claim to be a break-point of the British theatre. Alas, it had no banner title to wave and, after all, was in the East End poor relation theatre.

In summing up, I would say that *Look Back in Anger* showed a rebellion against the acceptance of a squalid life: *A Taste of Honey* showed an accep-tance of it. The former was more in tune with the needs of the age and a new drama: the latter was Chekhovian and, perhaps, although modern in approach, dated in intent.[2]

Jack's testimony is in accordance with the Brechtian desire of recent writers to look at this period in a new light and challenge the hegemony that has built up around John Russell Taylor's hugely influential work of

2. Jack Reading, Letter to the Author, 10 October 1997.

the sixties, *Anger and After*, the bible of the Angry Young Men Fan Club. Stephen Lacey's *British Realist Theatre* (1995) and, in particular, Charles Duff's *The Lost Summer: The Heyday of the West End Theatre* (1995) are both in this tradition, with Duff explicitly stating his revisionist intentions in his introduction, when he explains that

> My premise is simple: without underrating or denigrating the importance of any writer of the English Stage Company, many of their hypotheses about the state of the West End are wrong;...the standard of individual acting was high, and...its playwrights knew more about the human heart and wrote with greater literacy than many of their successors of the late 1950s and 1960s.

This historical *Verfremdung* is necessary, particularly as it is helping to reclaim the period between 1945 and 1954 from those who argue that it was a theatrical wasteland.

Events and personalities that I wish to highlight as significant in their own right, important for the subsequent development of British theatre and obscured by the clamour of the Angries are the foundation of the Arts Council; Binkie Beaumont and H.M. Tennent Ltd; the 1949 production of *A Streetcar Named Desire*; the Foreign Revelation; the interest in the French; musicals; the Festival of Britain; theatre critics; and Kenneth Tynan.

The metamorphosis of the Council for the Encouragement of Music and the Arts into the Arts Council of Great Britain on 9 August 1946 was an event of great significance for the theatrical health of the nation as a whole, in that it established the principle of state subsidy for the arts that was to underpin so much theatrical activity for the next 50 years. Early Arts Council grants encouraged, among other things, the foundation of the Bristol Old Vic in February 1946 and the emergence of repertory theatres in Guildford (1946), Ipswich (1947), Leatherhead (1951), Canterbury (1951) and Derby (1951). This renaissance of non-London venues provided a tremendous stimulus for regional theatre, and, in turn, created a new training ground for actors, directors, designers and technical staff, previously restricted to employment in the commercial sector. It also conferred greater freedom on producers to experiment with the programme, since the commercial imperative to stage safe and money-spinning works had to a partial extent been alleviated.

Prior to the advent of state subsidy, London and, in particular, West End theatre had been controlled by entrepreneurs dedicated to creating viable financial concerns. Pre-eminent amongst these was Hugh 'Binkie'

Beaumont, the managing director of H.M. Tennent Ltd, whose domination of the West End was hardly challenged in the 1940s. Purveying a house style that his biographer, Richard Hugget, defines as employing 'the greatest stars in gorgeous classic revivals amidst the most sumptuous settings which taste and money could devise',[3] Beaumont was responsible for some spectacular events: *Lady Windemere's Fan*, lavishly designed by Cecil Beaumont (1945); Emlyn Williams in Terence Rattigan's new work, *The Winslow Boy* (1946); the hugely popular American musical, *Oklahoma!* (1947), that so lit up the postwar gloom; Eileen Herlie in Jean Cocteau's *The Eagle Has Two Heads* (1947), which along with Christopher Fry's adaptation of Anouilh, *Ring Round the Moon* (1950), confirmed the increasing interest that British theatre was to have with all things French; and the highly controversial production of Tennessee Williams's *A Streetcar Named Desire* (1949), directed by Laurence Olivier and starring Vivien Leigh, to name just a few. Much of the polemic that was to sustain the new realist theatre after the advent of *Look Back in Anger* (1956) was predicated on an impassioned rejection of this very commercial success and, in particular, the values that Tennent's was alleged to embody—an obsession with glamour, a refusal to stage works that glanced at contemporary life or political concerns, a blind adherence to favoured house dramatists, such as Terence Rattigan and a continual representation of upper-middle class (and for realists, irrelevant) milieus. Coupled to the perception that Beaumont maintained a blacklist of actors who had crossed him that made it near impossible to obtain further work; the belief that Tennent's near domination of the West End stifled creativity; and the erroneous conviction that Beaumont, a discreet homosexual, only employed homosexual actors, it is easy to see how Beaumont was to become an important and inevitable Mephistopheles, fiendishly leading British theatre astray and memorably described by John Osborne as 'the most powerful of the unacceptable faeces of theatrical capitalism'.[4] A more objective assessment of this important figure is less clear cut. He undeniably paid poverty wages to all but his stars—Vivien Leigh received 10 per cent of the gross weekly box office receipts and a minimum of £175 per week for playing Blanche Dubois in the 1949 pro

---

3.   Richard Huggett, *Binkie Beaumont: Eminence Grise of the West End Theatre 1933–1973* (London: Hodder & Stoughton, 1989), p. 325.

4.   John Osborne, *Almost a Gentleman* (London: Faber & Faber, 1991), p. 20.

duction of *A Streetcar Named Desire*,[5] against the £5 per week offered to Frances St. Barbe-West for being the understudy to the part of Eunice and taking a walk-on role.[6] But for all his infamous parsimony Beaumont was nevertheless responsible for shows that still live in the memory of those that witnessed them, on account of the quality of their execution and the unparalleled lavishness that made them so diverting. This lavishness—which often embraced importing the latest Dior fashions from Paris for his leading ladies—necessarily contrasted strongly with postwar austerity and simultaneously enthralled and provoked. The ambiguity of theatrical attitudes in this period, an ambiguity encapsulated by Beaumont's productions, can be seen in the surprisingly flattering description of the young Kenneth Tynan—later to become the most vigorous champion of Kitchen-Sink drama, the antithesis of H.M. Tennent panache—of the impresario at the height of his power. In his 1953 'anthology of unique human beings' (with photographs by Cecil Beaton) entitled *Persona Grata*, Tynan was to write:

> With simple intentness, like a child setting out a doll's house, Beaumont enjoys arranging the theatre's affairs. Call him, if you like the image, an agile gnome with a genius for calculated risk... His basic gift repels definition. If questioned how he manages to bring the right men and the right moment into such unfailing theatrical collaboration, he raises an eyebrow, smiles a small, arcane smile, and says 'I hear curious drums beating...' Apart from a tendency to revive and overdress bad Victorian plays at the drop of a box-office receipt, he has been righter, on a higher level, than anyone else in the theatre of his time.[7]

How views would change.

Beaumont's power was in essence an economic one and it was to be weakened not by the advent of a new form of indigenous play, but by a change in government policy following the famous production of *A Streetcar Named Desire* in 1949.

Any discomfort that the increasingly beleaguered government of Clement Atlee, still reeling from the foreign exchange crisis of 1947, might have felt as a result of attacks on the work's alleged moral laxity (J.C. Trewin described it as a 'messy little anecdote') was exacerbated by the

5.   Vivien Leigh's contract for *A Streetcar Named Desire*, Papers Relating to H.M.Tennent Ltd, RP 95/2363, Theatre Museum, London.

6.   Osborne, *Almost a Gentleman*, p. 20.

7.   Kenneth Tynan and Cecil Beaton, 'Foreword', *Persona Grata* (London: Allan Wingate, 1953), p. vi.

row that developed over the decision of the recently created Arts Council to grant the play tax exemption on the grounds that it was partly cultural and partly educational. To offset the high cost of production (£10,000), the management, Tennent Productions Ltd, had turned itself into a non-profit making registered charity to avoid incurring Entertainment Tax (a 'temporary tax', introduced in 1916)—which, at 10 per cent of gross profits, had come to represent over a quarter of the price of a ticket by 1948.[8] This was a familiar practice on the part of theatrical managements, and in particular Tennent's, to take advantage of legislation that was originally designed to encourage straitened managers to stage more productions during the first world war. After the second world war, the Arts Council had appointed three officials, generally known as the Three Blind Mice, to rule on whether the plays claiming exemption could be classed as 'educational',[9] but this had little effect on Tennent's profitability—*A Streetcar Named Desire* was Tennent's fortieth such venture.[10]

On this occasion, however, Tennent's action was challenged by Members of Parliament in the House of Commons. When the Financial Secretary, Glenvil Hall, sought to explain that it was perfectly in order for the management to claim exemption on educational grounds, the Conservative Member for Brighton, A. Marlowe, asked whether the Minister was aware that 'this particular play is only educational to those who are ignorant of the facts of life?'[11] Needless to say, the play was to run at the Aldwych for 333 performances, but following an investigation by a Select Committee of the House of Commons into the practice of managements forming non-profit distributing subsidiaries in 1950—convened in the light of the furore surrounding *A Streetcar Named Desire*—the practice of the Arts Council of forming associations with commercial managements, to permit the latter to avoid Entertainment Tax, ceased and Tennent's became liable for income tax backdated to 1945. This was a not inconsiderable blow and represented the powerful company's first setback. It stressed that it was not omnipotent and would lead to the creation of literal space for new forms of drama, as its economic power lessened. All in all, a significant off-stage event.

8.   Simon Trussler, *The Cambridge Illustrated History of British Theatre* (Cambridge: Cambridge University Press, 1994), p. 303.

9.   Kitty Black, *Upper Circle* (London: Methuen, 1984), p. 154.

10.   Black, *Upper Circle*, p. 154.

11.   *Hansard* (London: HMSO, 1949), p. 2086.

The success of John Osborne's *Look Back in Anger* in 1956 has been seen by many as the crucial event that determined the reorientation of British theatre in the late 1950s ('If ever a revolution began with one explosion it was this'),[12] but, as with the closing of the Entertainment Tax loophole, there were other less visible milestones on the journey from stilted drawing-room drama to more diverse theatrical genres. The opening up after the war of the London stage to creative contact with New York and Paris, for example, was an event every bit of important for the evolution of twentieth-century English drama as the advent of Osborne, Wesker and the other 'new wave' dramatists. This fresh artistic contact introduced new techniques in acting, with Jean-Louis Barrault and the Comedie Française at the Edinburgh Festival in 1948 illustrating how English actors performed primarily with their voice, whilst their French counterparts utilized the entire body. Brecht's stress on the 'Gestus' of a performer, with body movement unlocking textual meaning, was to prove similarly illuminating. New ideas about acting and directing were absorbed by considering the work of Elia Kazan and the 'Method' technique developed by Lee Strasberg. The brash, glittering, technically perfect American musicals, symbolized by Rodgers and Hammerstein's smash hit, *Oklahoma!*, provoked English producers to consider more innovative ideas about stagecraft. Exposure to new types of plays by Sartre, Genet, Anouilh and Ionesco on the one hand, and Arthur Miller and Tennessee Williams on the other, provided a creative impulse that could not have been envisaged during the war and contact with new dramatic theories, such as French existentialist drama, and, later, Brecht's Epic Theatre, led a number of playwrights to applied these varied theatrical approaches to their own work. Although it is true to state that there was little new *English* writing between 1945 and 1955, it is disingenuous to conclude from this that the London theatre was a cultural wasteland, particularly given the rapidly growing interest in drama, borne out by the foundation of the first university drama department at Bristol in 1946, the establishment of learned groups such as the Society for Theatre Research (1948) and the proliferation of new drama periodicals, including *Theatre Notebook* (1946) and *Plays and Players* (1953). In many ways this ten-year period was crucial to the developments of the 1950s and the 1960s and were to make the English stage one of the most vibrant in the world, and it formed an important period of apprenticeship for actors, directors, playwrights and critics alike.

12. John Russell Taylor, *Anger and After* (London: Eyre Methuen, 1969), p. 14.

A particularly significant import was the musical. *Oklahoma!*'s success in 1947 trailed the way for several more important musicals up to 1954, predominately of American origin but occasionally British. These included *Annie Get Your Gun* (Coliseum, 1947), *Bless the Bride* (Adelphi, 1947, UK), *King's Rhapsody* (Palace, 1949, UK), *Carousel* (Drury Lane, 1950), *Kiss Me, Kate* (Coliseum, 1951), *South Pacific* (Drury Lane, 1950, UK), *Call Me Madam* (Coliseum, 1952), *Porgy and Bess* (Stoll, 1952), *The King and I* (Drury Lane, 1953), *Guys and Dolls* (Coliseum, 1953) and *Pal Joey* (Prince's, 1954). The appeal of the musicals for British audiences was matched only by the appeal of their profitability for theatre producers, as a letter from Lawrence Langner, the Director of the Theatre Guild in New York, to Binkie Beaumont makes clear in 1951:

> I thought you would enjoy reading the rave notices that *Oklahoma!* received when it returned to New York. It is now packing them in in an enormous theater, the Broadway, which would correspond to Stoll's Opera House. We have kept the prices the same, and it is going to gross more than it did originally. This shows that you can bring back *Oklahoma!* to London after three years on the road.[13]

Whether a licence to print money or not (adumbrating the West End in the 1980s and 1990s), the sheer proliferation of the genre on the London stage at this time does, however, refute the notion that this was a glamour starved period for the London stage.

1950 was to prove the year of the French play on the London stage, albeit in translation. At the beginning of the new decade the most popular domestic dramatist was Christopher Fry. In January 1950 he was enjoying unparalleled success, with three of his plays running simultaneously in the West End—*Venus Observ'd* (starring Laurence Olivier as the Duke of Altair), *The Lady's Not for Burning* (concluding an eight-month run at the Globe) and an early religious work, *The Boy with a Cart* (at the Lyric). The appetite for what he termed his 'sliced prose' (a term that emphasizes the linguistic dexterity of his works) seemed unquenchable. A fourth Fry work, appearing in February at the Globe, marked a new departure in that it was not only in prose but was also a translation of Jean Anouilh's *L'Invitation au Chateau*, renamed Ring *Round the Moon*. The work was significant in that it convinced many that as well as being intellectually stimulating, new French drama could be entertaining in a less uncompromising manner.

---

13. Papers relating to H.M. Tennent, 95/2363, Theatre Museum.

Although Terence Rattigan created *The Browning Version* (1948), a brilliant psychological depiction of the academic and personal failure of a deeply disliked school-master, such intelligent works were increasingly perceived as the exceptions that proved the rule, the rule being that it was the foreign imports that were exciting, innovative and daring. The much heralded *Death of a Salesman* by Arthur Miller demonstrated how it was American playwrights who dared to scrutinize contemporary society (London, 1950)—as far as political satire was concerned, the London theatre seemed hermetically sealed—and at the beginning of the decade another tranche of musicals arrived to irk the critics and thrill the public. Whilst J.C.Trewin felt *Carousel* (1950) to be 'sophistication crossed with bland innocence',[14] Ivor Brown loathed the 'sex-hunger' of the sailors in *South Pacific* (1950) 'peeping, from their iron prison, through binoculars at girls undressing on shore'[15] and Harold Hobson reviled *Kiss Me, Kate* (1951) for containing jokes that are 'humiliatingly naïve',[16] the public ignored this collective primness and flocked in their thousands to witness these fanfares of colour, light, music and vigour—attributes in short supply in a country still enduring rationing. Up until *Porgy and Bess* (1952) there was a strict embargo on the playing of the tunes from these shows, a marketing ploy that helped stimulate voracious interest in their arrival, and John Elsom, a young man at the time, reflects the immense appeal of these new musicals somewhat more accurately than then critics who were yearning for a more intellectual revival, when he writes:

> ...when I first started to go to the theatre regularly, in the early 1950s, an evening at an American musical was usually one of sheer delight, not unmixed with a sense of guilty awareness that I went to see Shakespeare or Eliot at the Old Vic in a spirit of dutiful respect.[17]

Dutiful respect was to become an increasingly unfashionable commodity in the 1950s.

The Festival of Britain which took place in London in 1951 was designed to convey a similar impression of stability, being both an affirmation that Britons had emerged from the trials of the immediate postwar period and a showcase for British art and technology. Sponsored by the Labour government, just prior to the end of its administration, it gave

14. 'Old Acquaintance', *Observer*, 23 July 1950.
15. 'Very Blue Waters', *Observer*, 23 July 1950.
16. 'Derivations', *Sunday Times*, 11 March 1951.
17. John Elsom, *Post-War British Theatre Criticism* (London: Routledge & Kegan Paul, 1981), p. 39.

architects the platform to demonstrate their renewed vigour, be it in the construction of the concert venue, the Festival Hall, the National Film Theatre or the esoteric pleasure gardens at Battersea.[18] As far as the theatre was concerned, however, it provided visible proof that the country contained superlative actors and actresses, but regrettably few new durable vehicles in which they could perform. The appearance of Edith Evans, Sybil Thorndike, and Wendy Hiller together on N.C. Hunter's *Waters of the Moon* was a memorable event, but it was hard for some observers to escape the feeling that this 'planetary cast'[19] turned the dramatist's text into something more substantial than he had actually conceived. Vivien Leigh's performance as Cleopatra alongside her husband, Laurence Olivier, as Antony at the St James's Theatre (May 1951) moved Ivor Brown 'almost beyond endurance at the close'[20] and John Gielgud's Stratford Leontes, in *The Winter's Tale* directed by Peter Brook, was a revelation, hailed as 'actual, exciting, believable, pathetic, a man and not the emanation of a fantasy'.[21] Indeed, there now seemed to be no male Shakespearean role that Gielgud could not rescue from critical or academic indifference. But the fact remained that there appeared to be a danger of a 'bardic traffic jam'[22] in the West End, a danger realized in 1953, when Harold Hobson alone reviewed 24 different productions of Shakespeare plays in that year, with four separate openings in the first week of July.

What is perhaps most noticeable about the London stage between 1952 and 1954 is how completely indifferent it was to contemporary events. The heavy costs of a rearmament programme necessitated by the Korean war; the inflationary pressures that this produced in a still war-weakened country; the continued shortages caused by rationing; the dramatic impact of the welfare state; the two elections of 1951, which resulted in an elderly Churchill regaining power for the Conservatives; the spectre of Cold War conflagration; and the manufacture of the first British nuclear bomb failed to impinge upon the West End stage at all. There were brief glimmerings of alternative works—a group called Theatre Workshop staged Uranium 235 in 1952, although the relevance of its subject

18. Henry Pelling, *Modern Britain: 1885–1955* (London: Nelson, 1965), pp. 187-88.
19. Ivor Brown, 'Trips to the Moors', *Observer*, 22 April 1951.
20. 'The Lass Unparalleled', *Observer*, 13 May 1951.
21. Ivor Brown, 'In Gay Bohemia', *Observer*, 1 July 1951.
22. Ivor Brown, 'Greater and Less', *Observer*, 10 February 1951.

matter was dismissed as propaganda—but genuinely ground-breaking work was too often deemed perplexing. This was most apparent in Ivor Brown's tentative response to John Whiting's *Marching Song*, in April 1954: 'Mr Whiting writes with energy and originality, but what exactly he intends to say, playgoers must decide for themselves'.[23]

The unadventurous nature of the West End mirrored the constrictions of early 1950s society. A contemporaneous description of the then Lord Chamberlain appearing in the *Observer* in 1952, helps convey a powerful flavour of the period:

> Lord Clarendon enjoys shooting and fishing, despite a heavy limp acquired in a childhood accident. He lives as he was brought up to live, surrounded by his treasured Van Dycks, well and happily married, performing his difficult office with charm and skill[24]

and it was this stratification through class of the theatre, the plethora of Shakespeare, the continued dominance of H.M.Tennent's, the obsession with the French and the avoidance of matters political that became a source of deep frustration for one man in particular, Kenneth Tynan.

The sheer brilliance of Tynan's observations in late 1954 and 1955 not only provided a revelatory diagnosis of the reasons for the theatre's stasis, but gave a hint of the excitement to come, and ushered in a new golden age of theatre criticism. Tynan, who had previously been a dandy at Oxford, a failed actor and director before becoming a theatre critic for the *Evening Standard*, succeeded Ivor Brown at the *Observer* in September 1954. He immediately gave notice of his polemical intent:

> I see myself predominantly as a lock. If the key, which is the work of art, fits snugly into my mechanism of bias and preference, I click and rejoice; if not, I am helpless, and can only offer the artist the address of a better locksmith... It is a sombre truth that nowadays our intellectuals go to the cinema and shun the theatre. Their assistance is sadly missed; but their defection is my opportunity.[25]

Young (he was 27 on his appointment), attuned to the dissatisfaction of his own generation, fashionably left of centre and a lover of American musicals, Tynan was, above all, a stylish, captivating writer. Observations ranging from the refreshingly direct:

23. 'Guessing Game', *Observer*, 11 April 1954.
24. Anon, 'Profile: The Lord Chamberlain', *Observer*, 10 February 1952.
25. 'Ins and Outs', *Observer*, 5 September 1954.

> Twenty seven West End theatres are at present offering light comedies and musical shows of which perhaps a dozen are good of their kind. The number of new plays with a claim to serious discussion is three... One need not be a purist to be ashamed of the discrepancy[26]

to the fiercely didactic:

> Night-nurses at the bed-side of good drama, we critics keep a holy vigil. Black circles rim our eyes as we pray for the survival of our pet patient, starved and racked, the theatre of passion and ideas.[27]

From the devastatingly witty, such as the famous pastiche of Terence Rattigan's *Separate Tables*, that constituted a review at the end of September 1954,[28] to the lasceratingly descriptive, most notably his denunciation of the typical West End work, set in the fictional Home County of Loamshire, where

> [the] inhabitants belong to a social class derived partly from romantic novels and partly from the playwright's vision of the leisured life he will lead after the play is a success—this being the only effort of imagination he is called on to make[29]

all seemed to provide the excitement so patently missing from the West End itself. He gave hints of important theatrical movements in Europe, such as Brecht's Epic Theatre, and lamented the theatre world's ignorance of their significance—'We in London hear the distant thunder of the guns: but how shall we judge of the outcome?'[30] He welcomed the relevance and innovation of Theatre Workshop's *The Good Soldier Schweik*—'With half a dozen replacements, Theatre Workshop might take London by storm'[31]—and he lambasted Britain's social, political and cultural insularity, which he saw as embracing fear of America, fear of the advent of commercial television, fear of criticism, fear of emotional engagement, fear of an open sexuality and a fear enforced by censors of film and theatre, who both discouraged political attacks on the establishment.[32]

26. 'The Second Rate', *Observer*, 19 September 1954,

27. 'The Lost Art of Bad Drama', *A View of the English Stage* (London: Methuen, 1984), p. 149.

28. 'Mixed Double', *Observer*, 26 September 1954.

29. 'West End Apathy', *Observer*, 31 October 1954.

30. 'Dead Language', *Observer*, 21 November 1954.

31. 'Pogrom Notes', *Observer*, 14 November 1954.

32. Kathleen Tynan, *The Life of Kenneth Tynan* (London: Methuen, 1988), p. 116.

By the mid-decade, Tynan's writing had touched a nerve in many. *Plays and Players*, in its end of year report, 'Credits and Discredits for 1954' had three simple wishes for 1955: 'Better plays, better acting, better productions'.[33] Acerbic, prejudicial, unfair and compelling, in the four months to the end of 1954, Tynan had offered several prescriptions for 'the theatre of passion and ideas'. The question now remained: who would administer the cure?

33. Peter Roberts (ed.), *The Best of Plays and Players 1953–1968* (London: Methuen, 1988), p. 42.

Foreign Drama and the Lord Chamberlain in the 1950s

Steve Nicholson

In 1951, a member of the public wrote to the Lord Chamberlain to complain about the fact that *A Streetcar Named Desire* had been licensed for public performance. In his reply, he defended the decision as follows:

> The Censor of Plays has the unenviable task of holding a balance for the general public as a whole, between those who are surprised that such-and-such a play has been licensed and those who are astonished that there should be any doubt about it being passed... If the Play Censorship exerted its powers to such an extent that the Theatre ceased to be a mirror of contemporary life, apart from causing great hardship to the entertainment world, it would do irrevocable harm to the future study of this epoch. It is not the task of the Censor of Plays to ensure that the public get 'pleasant and satisfactory entertainment'.[1]

I start with that quotation both because we are now from that future seeking to study the epoch in question, and because it seems to set out a surprisingly liberal and responsible position. Indeed, his correspondent wrote again to say that she now identified the Lord Chamberlain as one of the major obstacles to the crucial reforming work of the Public Morality Council.

The Lord Chamberlain's statement invites us, of course, to measure the practice against such a reasonable sounding theory. But in an attack on theatre censorship in 1958, the *Sunday Times* described the recent activities of what it called 'this quaint and dangerous institution' as 'thirteen months' work without parallel even in its own long and ridiculous history. We are now rapidly approaching a situation', the newspaper suggested, 'in which a dramatist will hear that his play has been

---

1. Unless otherwise stated, all quotations are taken from the Lord Chamberlain's Correspondence Files, now housed in the Manuscript Section of the British Library. Material is filed under play titles.

licensed with disgust and despondency. It will practically be a guarantee that his work is feeble minded.'[2]

While British writers did not escape censorship, I have chosen to focus on foreign plays for two particular reasons. First, one of the features of British theatre in the 1950s was the influx and the influence of a number of significant foreign dramatists, including Brecht, Ionesco, Sartre, Genet, Tennessee Williams, Miller and Samuel Beckett. Second, it is undoubtedly the case that before the Second World War theatre censorship had often been most oppressive in relation to foreign plays, with the Lord Chamberlain's Office making frequent disparaging references to those few British theatre producers who sought to bring foreign plays into British culture. *Miss Julie*—a 'filthy piece' which 'all public opinion that is worth consideration looks to the censor to protect them from'—is one example of a play which suffered.[3] For most British playwrights, on the other hand, censorship worked effectively as a hidden force, since they were not likely to spend time writing plays that would not receive licences in their own country; their non-existent works are the 'unborn children' referred to by a critic of censorship in the 1930s, and the Lord Chamberlain was the contraceptive.[4]

While the pre-war censors had claimed that the supposedly lower moral standards and coarser tastes of other nations had to be resisted, their actions had more often prevented serious subjects—political and philosophical—as well as more experimental forms from entering pre-war British theatre. In testing the response to the challenges of postwar foreign dramatists, Sartre's *Huis Clos*, first submitted in 1945 but not licensed for performance till 1959, is therefore an appropriate place to start. The first application to the Lord Chamberlain was from the British Council on behalf of a French company planning to perform it in French on a tour of Britain. 'How typical it is of the French mentality and attitude', sneered one of the Lord Chamberlain's advisers, and the Reader's report makes the main objection more explicit:

2.   The *Sunday Times*, 9 February, 1958.

3.   See my discussion of this in Steve Nicholson, 'Unnecessary Plays: European Drama and the British Censor', *Theatre Research International* 20.1 (1995), pp. 30-36.

4.   In 1934, Hubert Griffith, the playwright and critic, wrote of the ' "unborn children"—the plays that a generation of intelligent young dramatists might have liked to have written but had been warned that they must not write.' See Dorothy Knowles, *The Censor, the Drama and the Film 1900–1934* (London: G. Allen and Unwin, 1934), p. 4.

The play illustrates very well the difference between the French and English tastes. I don't suppose that anyone would bat an eyelid over in Paris, but here we bar Lesbians on the stage… Sartre is all the rage amongst the Intelligentsia at the moment…but it would need a clever advocate to persuade me that British culture needs the introduction of such queer themes from the continent for its healthy life.

Striking, too, is the the arrogance with which the Reader dismisses Sartre's philosophy, and thereby excuses the censors from the charge that anything of significance was being banned. 'The play', he said, 'presents only one side' and

totally ignores the possibility of a redemption either by faith or works. This failure to develop completely a theme which must stand or fall by its metaphysical verity makes it easier to withold performance on the obvious grounds…of eroticism and Lesbianism, without feeling that an important work of art is being stifled.

Despite many requests from professional and amateur companies wishing to perform Sartre's play—including one by the Meterological Office of the Air Ministry who wished to enter it for a competition in Dunstable—the Lord Chamberlain felt bound to refuse a public performance 'so long as the ban on perversion exists'. He admitted that it might 'appear anomalous' that the play could be broadcast on the Radio and not staged, but observed that

there is a difference between words coming over the air and the same words spoken in the more personal atmosphere of a theatre by visible characters…many people who listened to the broadcast of the play did not notice the perversion…whereas this particular thing was quite apparent when produced in the theatre.

Lillian Hellmann's 1930s play about lesbianism, *The Children's Hour*, also remained banned until 1960, though several would-be producers in the 1950s were prepared to go to almost any lengths in making changes. The Lord Chamberlain told them that

I am afraid the only alteration you could make in this play would be to substitute for the lesbianism some more normal vice—such as dope or men.

In the case of Genet's *The Maids* in 1952, the censors were relieved that the implicit lesbian element gave them a justification for banning a play which 'though written with a certain hysterical power' was 'horrible, deeply decadent and morbid' and therefore 'quite unsuited…to public performance before mixed audiences'. But the examiner acknowledged that

> as the point at which mere decadence in itself is sufficient to incur the refusal of a licence is a difficult and delicate matter to determine, I am cowardly enough to welcome the definite indications of Lesbianism which simplify my task.

In terms of homosexuality, it was, ironically, Arthur Miller's *A View From The Bridge* which created the most hostile press for the Lord Chamberlain in the mid 1950s, primarily because of the publicity generated when Miller and, more importantly, Marilyn Monroe, came to London to attend what was officially a private performance. Part of the irony is that the Lord Chamberlain had been relatively sympathetic to the play when it was first submitted: 'Unlike Mr. Tennessee Williams, whose neuroses grin through everything he writes, Mr. Miller's work is always objective'.

However, he demanded 'the deletion of that small action where Eddie kisses the boy' since this carried 'too forceful a homosexual implication', and the refusal to make this cut led to the play being banned from public performance.

In theory, there was no political censorship in the theatre of the 1950s, and if we turn to the writer whose work was most explicitly and obviously political, Bertolt Brecht, it is true that the cuts made were almost exclusively to do with swearing or sex or religion. The politics were not liked—in licensing *The Caucasian Chalk Circle* for the RSC in 1962 the Examiner found it 'rather pitiful that direct Communist propaganda should be produced by the Company (under the patronage of the Queen) which will be the nucleus of our future National Theatre'—but they were effectively untouched. In 1953, when *The Good Woman of Setzuan* was first submitted, only one change ('bum' for 'arse') was demanded, and the play's political line was sufficiently vague to be both patronised and misunderstood. In the eyes of the Lord Chamberlain's reader, the moral dilemma posed by the play is 'How can we mortals be both good and rich', and the playwright was praised not only for presenting 'the unusual spectacle of a Communist in a tolerably good temper' but also for being

> inclined to blame human nature…rather than 'the system' for the evils of the world. It is too much of a strain for him to keep this up for more than two thirds of the way through, and at the end we have conventional sweat-shop and trial scenes, but I suppose this is inevitable.

In fact, *The Threepenny Opera* was the play of Brecht which most irritated them, and though only minor cuts were imposed, there was an obviously political and nationalistic dimension to their resentment of a German 'coarsening' of a 'charming' piece of theatre.

> While there may be justification in varying so specifically English a piece for foreign consumption, there can be little or none in retranslating this hodge podge into English, when we have the original *Beggar's Opera* itself... I hope it chokes them.

In 1955, a dozen cuts were imposed on *Mother Courage*, but they are again not to do with the main thrust of the play. The censors' view of the playwright here was that

> in a generally acceptable denunciation of the horrors of war, he is able to slip in a good deal of the Communist Party line, indulging its religious aspects, in a manner that would scarcely be censorable even in a country where the stage censorship was political in its nature.

Yet although the term 'sexual politics' may not have existed in the 1950s, so years on we can no longer so easily divide moral from political censorship. Recent revelations about the British government's treatment of homosexuals at this time make the blanket ban on stage references unsurprising, and this policy persisted until 1958, the year after publication of the Wolfenden report. 'A careful consideration of the homosexual element' was demanded when *Cat on a Hot Tin Roof* was submitted in 1955, but in fact sexuality of all sorts caused problems. Over 40 specific cuts were made to Tennessee Williams's play, but more than 20 of these remained even after the ban on homosexual references was lifted. The original Reader's Report identified 'the author's horror, disgust and rage against the sexual act' and patronisingly proclaimed that 'once again Mr. Williams vomits up the recurring theme of his not-too-subconscious'. When most of the homosexual references were restored in 1958, a somewhat more sympathetic Examiner suggested that

> The play undoubtedly qualifies as 'serious and sincere'. Twisted as is much of Mr Williams's psychology and disagreeable and disgusting as are his oversized characters...he feels passionately about them and about using the dramatist's art to probe and expound their problems.

Yet as late as 1967, 26 cuts were imposed by an Examiner who was reluctant to accept that the climate had changed:

> In my opinion, time has not made all that difference. The obscenities noted in the original remain obscenities... I still believe him to be patho-

logically biased and to possess an inflated sense of his own importance.

There was much to censor, too, in the 'pathalogical nastiness' of *The Balcony* by 'the unspeakable Monsieur Genet'.

> The Lord Chamberlain would be prepared to consider giving a licence to this Play if the major themes of blasphemy and perversion were eradicated. He would also require the deletion of the castration episode and the matter of the phallus in Act II. In addition words such as bugger would have to be altered and the constant references to brothels and whores reduced.

Even when numerous cuts to lines and changes to action had been made, the sound effect representing off-stage flagellation remained a sticking point. One production proposed substituting a piece of music, but was told that

> The Lord Chamberlain considers that there is so little difference between a woman's scream and 'a high pitched and intense' burst of music that he is not prepared to allow what you have suggested. He would, on the other hand, be prepared to consider…furniture being knocked over.

The censors were keen whenever possible to avoid admitting to having banned plays completely, and it is true that relatively few were refused the possibility of a licence in any circumstances. But it is surely twisting the truth to say that a play on which dozens of cuts have been imposed is free and that the blame for it not being licensed falls on the playwright who refuses to compromise. The censors invariably insisted that any playwright who resisted their demands was being unreasonable and arrogant. In 1957, for example, the Lord Chamberlain famously refused to grant a licence to the English version of Samuel Beckett's *Endgame*, because one of the characters, having prayed unsuccessfully to God, remarks 'the bastard—he doesn't exist'. This, in fact, was the clash which provoked the attack on the censors by the *Sunday Times*, which I mentioned earlier. To the *Sunday Times*, Beckett was 'one of the greatest, the most serious and the noblest playwrights of our time', and this play 'one of the chief works of one of the chief writers of our age' which the censorship had effectively banned. 'How long shall we endure not being allowed to see it?' asked the paper. The Lord Chamberlain's Examiner agreed to a private meeting with the play's proposed producer, George Devine, and recorded his version of the meeting:

> I stressed that the Lord Chamberlain had not banned the play, but only required a small alternation which could be made with no detriment to

the play if its author was not a conceited ass. If they put it about that the play had been banned we should do our best to prove them liars.

Six months later the Lord Chamberlain was still writing: 'Let us hope that Beckett will come to his senses—and alter one word—which he can so easily do'.

Yet perhaps what is more surprising now than the dismissive attitude of the Lord Chamberlain's office towards playwrights is the extent to which opponents of censorship were apparently prepared to sacrifice their principles and say whatever they judged necessary to persuade the Lord Chamberlain to change his mind. This is what George Devine wrote to the Lord Chamberlain about the 'blasphemous remark' of *Endgame*:

> In my opinion, and that I think of others, this is a profoundly moral play, and in view of the fact that Clov's answer to Hamm's comment 'He doesn't exist' are the word's 'Not yet', the dramatist is implying that man is not yet worthy of God, but that he should become worthy, and that part of the message of the play is that if man made an effort to earn God, he would then be worthy of Him.

Devine then promised he would be 'bringing pressure to bear' on the playwright, relying on 'Beckett's vanity, which will make him desire London production when his original pettish reaction to the banning of his play has subsided'.

What seemed to give the situation over *Endgame* an absurdity beyond even that intended by its author, was that the play had already been performed in the same theatre in French. Though the Examiner had picked up some obscenities in the French text, he had had little hesitation in granting a licence: 'Though I detest this pretentious rubbish worse than death or the taxes, there is otherwise no reason why it should not be licensed.'

In fact, licensing a play in a foreign language which was then refused in English translation had plenty of precedents—it had happened, for example, with Pirandello's *Six Characters in Search of an Author*—but a number of newspapers were quick to pick up the discrepancy now as a way of attacking the censors. As the Lord Chamberlain told his officials:

> We are being stoned a little over the play *Endgame or Fin de Partie*. I feel that people erudite enough to go, understanding, to a French play can take a great deal more dirt (I use the term broadly) than an average English audience seeing a direct translation in English. Quite apart from the fact that the French words sound more delicate than the English equivalent.

It was not Hamm's denial of the existence of God which was considered blasphemous, but the fact that he called him a bastard. 'Unhappily, of course,' wrote the Lord Chamberlain, 'we did let him blaspheme in French!' The embarrassed Reader who had passed that script expressed his 'deep apology to Lord Scarborough for having unwittingly but negligently placed him in a position of apparent inconsistency', through not having detected the issue in the French text:

> Beckett is horrid and difficult stuff because so inconsequent, and more so in French, but I should have been warned by the fact that the earlier *Waiting for Godot* also contained blasphemy, though this was excised without public complaint from management or author.

In fact, the licensing of *Waiting for Godot* had not been quite so straightforward as this implies. Some predictable cuts had been demanded—references to arses, to farting, to sexual diseases and to the 'secondary effect of hanging'. But the Reader was also worried that he could 'detect distinct mockery of religion' both in Lucky's speech and in Estragon's comparison of himself to Christ. Beckett himself wrote a letter reluctantly agreeing to amend most of the passages causing problems, but insisted that the biblical references were crucial:

> I am prepared to try and give satisfaction on ten of the twelve points raised. This for me is a big concession and I make it with the greatest reluctance. Were it not for my desire to be agreeable to Mr Glenville and yourself, I should simply call the whole thing off without further discussion. But two of the passages condemned...are vital to the play and can neither be suppressed nor changed. I cannot conceive in what they give offence and I consider their interdiction wholly unreasonable. I am afraid this is quite final.

Beckett's stand won reluctant concessions, but the Lord Chamberlain reasserted his authority by rejecting some of the playwright's other amendments to censored passages. For example, the playwright's substitution for 'who farted' of 'who did that?' was not accepted: 'NO. There is no need for this. The Lord Chamberlain should stand firm about any business of breaking wind.'

After the production transferred with success to the West End, the Lord Chamberlain received a letter expressing disgust and disbelief that the play had been licensed:

> Lady Howitt presents her compliments to the Lord Chamberlain. She wishes to inform him that she visited the Criterion Theatre with her husband and that both were completely disgusted by the play *Waiting for*

Godot. They cannot understand how such a production can possibly get through the British procedure of censorship.

> The play itself is sordid, bestial and brutal...one of the main themes running through the play is the desire of two old tramps continually to relieve themselves. Such a dramatisation of lavatory necessities is offensive and against all sense of British decency.

The Lord Chamberlain ordered one of his staff to go and see the production: 'I dare say they are doing all sorts of filthy things by now. There are plenty of opportunities in the script.'

His Examiner found the specific accusation unfounded and suggested that public opinion be allowed 'to disperse this ugly little jet of marsh gas'. In a polite rely to Lady Howitt, he expressed regret that it was impossible to ban the play:

> It was submitted to this Office early this year clearly with some trepidation: and quite rightly, because the original was appalling, and some of the more outrageous passages were deleted, much to the author's rage. What is left is unpleasant enough but the Lord Chamberlain felt that to cut more would be tantamount to banning the whole production.

Lady Howitt was not satisfied, and wrote again:

> I am perturbed to think what may follow if a play such as this is allowed and I do wish that two of the incidents could yet be omitted. The first is when one of the tramps goes into the wing and the other tramp and the big capitalist both watch the man in the wings making remarks about what he is doing. This I thought extremely objectionable. The second incident was when one of the tramps ran along the stage until he reached the tree in the centre of the stage when he evidently pretended to do what I never expected to see on any English stage, although a French audience might find it amusing.

Even when the Royal Court staged the play in 1964, the licence contained an endorsement stating that 'At no point during the action of the play must there be any miming of urination or excretion on stage'.

As this last example shows, visual images were as important as words. The actor manager of a 1953 touring production of Sartre's *The Respectable Prostitute* was prosecuted in court and heavily fined for a final image in which a man carried a woman to a bed and began to lie on top of her as the curtain fell. The Lord Chamberlain was able to say that because this action had not been specified in the script it was therefore unlicensed, and, to his relief, the press united behind him in condemning the liberty taken by the production—surely an impossible and impractical position to maintain, since it implies that no production may include any stage action not written into the script.

In *Godot*, the stage direction requiring Estragon to have 'his hand pressed to his pubis' had to be modified, and the Censors also debated the incident where Estragon's trousers fall down. 'Better keep them up' wrote one official; 'Leave provided he is well covered', wrote his superior.

In Tennessee Williams's *The Rose Tattoo*, a design note specifying that a character be 'clad only in a sheer white slip' concerned the Examiners. 'According to the dictionary, "sheer" means diaphanous, but perhaps feminine advice is needed', wrote one Reader. 'Non-diaphanous, please', added the Lord Chamberlain.

In the same play, the Examiner was mortified to discover through an 'anonymous correspondent' that he had failed to recognize a 'rubber preventative' which falls out of a character's pocket, and an endorsement had to be applied after the play had been running for some time:

> This is a good example of the difference between seeing and reading a play, however trained may be the powers of visualization... I did not associate the passage with the possibility of a French letter, thinking the object some Sicilian love talisman or the like. None the less I am humiliated, and offer my apologies...

Despite what some examples might seem to imply, I would question the easy assumption that the Lord Chamberlain and his officials in the 1950s were little more than a bunch of incompetent fools. Indeed, such a misjudgment actually lets them off the hook. Censors are often accused of being humourless—but in fact there is often wit in the responses and memoranda of the Lord Chamberlain's office. When the Reader of *Krapp's Last Tape* dismissively observed that 'Mr Beckett's mind is like a mournful decayed public convenience in which elderly smelly men... defecate the standing pool of thought' the Lord Chamberlain wrote in the margin 'Copy to Mr Beckett!!' I suspect that even when the cuts and alterations may seem ridiculous, they are often quite deliberately and maliciously satirizing the supposed pretensions of the playwrights.

The quality of Readers and Examiners varied, but some clearly read the plays very sharply, understanding much of what was going on, and making sometimes imaginative anticipations of what the performance might do with the text. The Examiner who first read *Waiting for Godot* concluded his report with the following analysis:

I will venture tentatively the following interpretation. The play is a modern cry of despair, and Godot, for whom we human tramps are always waiting in expectation, is Death. Pozzo and Lucky are allegorical figures passing before our eyes of how men treat one another, by acts of enslavement that lead to blindness for the enslaver and dumbness for the slave. The best way out is a piece of rope—what Shakespeare called 'the charity of a penny cord'.

Sometimes, as here, the Examiners' ability to interpret a play and their alertness to implicit meanings is more impressive than the responses of theatre critics who have actually had the chance to see the play in performance. Referring to the visual image at the end of Ionesco's *The Lesson*, the Reader's Report confidently identifies the play as 'a clumsy allegory of the sexual act', and this perception leads directly to the need to censor the ending:

> though it may kill the whole play I think the Lord Chamberlain will agree with me that the body of the girl must not fall into an immodest position, that the professor must not stand (as he cannot fail to do if the stage directions are followed) between her legs to deliver the second blow, and that the second blow must not in any circumstances resemble the male sexual act.

The endorsement therefore read as follows:

> This licence is issued on the understanding that the following alterations are made—
> 1. p.50, the Stage Direction 'then falls, crumpling into an immodest position', to be altered, so that there is nothing immodest in the position of the girl.
> 2. p.51. The girl must not have her legs apart as described in the stage direction, and the thrust of the knife must not be in any way suggestive.

Perhaps the role of buffoon was rather one which it was sometimes convenient for the Lord Chamberlain to play.

It is unfair to criticize or judge the censorship and the Lord Chamberlain in isolation. There is no doubt that he received plenty of letters and pressures to be more as well as less draconian in his decisions, and the Public Morality Council could be active and forceful on occasions. On the other hand, by and large the Censors seem to have been more out of step with more of the press in the 1950s than had been the case before the war. In reluctantly licensing Sartre's *The Respectable Prostitute* in 1958, the Lord Chamberlain acknowledged that 'Mrs Partington and Canute were both wrong'. The tide would take another 10 years to come in, and many of the 'new waves' would flow from British playwrights. But the pressure created by the work of foreign dramatists was highly significant in helping to breach the defences.

Terence Rattigan: The Voice of the 1950s

Christopher Innes

Rattigan has had an unusually, indeed undeservedly bad press. Ever since the 1950s his work has been treated with critical disdain. He is almost always represented as the potentially serious playwright who sold out to popularity; who substituted craftsmanship for vision, dealing (one critic as early as 1953 remarked) 'less in terms of observed life than in those of observed theatre'.[1] Undeniably, there's a certain truth in all that. However, on a quite different level, Rattigan's plays express the essential quality of English society as a whole in the 1950s. The deeper, conceptual structure of his drama can be seen as embodying dominant aspects in social consciousness of the time; and on this level even the obliquity and apparent refusal of challenging reality, for which he was attacked, have representative value.

Looking back on English theatre from the vantage-point of the end of the century, it might seem wilfully eccentric to call Terence Rattigan the 'voice of the 1950s'. After all, Bernard Shaw's death in 1950 effectively marked the end of a theatrical era. And in the mid-1950s came a revolution in British drama: one that Rattigan explicitly fought against. This radical shift was fuelled by the innovations of Sam Beckett and the belated influence of Brecht—both of which Rattigan attacked. The strident voice of this revolution, of course, was John Osborne—whose plays Rattigan disliked, however generous his public comments. However, it is all too easy for theatre-historians to mistake a change in the tone and subject-matter of drama for change in society at large. In fact there was a significant disjunction between events on the stage (particularly the stage of the Royal Court), and the state of affairs outside the

---

1. George Jean Nathan, *Theatre Arts*, January 1953, p. 21.

theatre. The major changes that reshaped the political landscape of post-war Britain, and provided a social consensus that survived more or less intact right up to the Thatcher era, had already taken place in the 1940s. During the 1950s in particular English society stayed very much in a holding pattern—and Rattigan remained writing exactly the same kind of plays as he had in the previous decade. From one perspective it is precisely this that makes his drama representative of the period, even as it made his drama seem dated to critics who recognized, and promoted the new theatrical wave.

After *Look Back in Anger* in 1956, anger, youth, authenticity and working-class experience were the new critical touchstones—while Rattigan, as the most successful West End playwright of the time, was clearly on the wrong side: the self-declared representative of the discredited establishment to be strung up from the nearest lamppost. Indeed, to a large degree the new wave of English dramatists defined themselves in direct reaction against Rattigan. For instance, it was outraged disgust at seeing Margaret Leighton wasting her talents in Rattigan's *Variations on a Theme*, that moved Shelagh Delany (still a schoolgirl in 1958) to write her first play, *A Taste of Honey*. Ten years later Rattigan was just as much a target for John Arden and Margaretta D'Arcy, whose choice of Nelson as a symbol of oppression in their 1968 play, *The Hero Rises Up*, was in conscious opposition to Rattigan's 1966 television-drama, *Nelson: A Portrait in Miniature*. And Ken Tynan, the critical spokesman for the new wave, singled Rattigan out as 'the Formosa of the contemporary theatre, occupied by the old guard'.[2] Even though Tynan went on to say that Rattigan might also be 'geographically inclined towards the progressives', that implied he was not simply a reactionary, but a traitor to the cause.

It might even seem a gratuitous example of black humour to identify Rattigan with the 1950s—since Rattigan greeted the decade with a series of public statements, which set him graphically at odds with his contemporaries in the theatre, and handed his critics the ammunition that forced his work almost completely off the stage in the 1960s.

The first of these statements was an article he published in March 1950, attacking the 'Play of Ideas' and asserting that 'from Aeschylus to Tennessee Williams the only theatre that matters is the theatre of charac-

2.   Kenneth Tynan, 'The Lost Art of Bad Drama' (1955), reprinted in *idem*, *Curtains* (London: Longmans, 1961), p. 91.

ter and narrative'.[3] This provoked the immediate response that Rattigan's argument showed his own plays (supposedly solely 'about people')[4]
as anything but non-political: as one critic remarked, 'Equate Character
with Right thinking and Idea with Subversive thinking, and you begin
to appreciate what Mr Rattigan is trying to say'.[5] Then, when the first
two volumes of his *Collected Plays* were published in 1953, Rattigan used
the prefaces to defend his plays on the basis of their public success, as
'middlebrow entertainment', specifically written for a popular audience
he characterized as 'Aunt Edna'—'a nice, respectable, middle-class, mid-
dle-aged, maiden lady'.[6] All too naturally, 'Aunt Edna' was read as a
close relation of Mrs Grundy, the prurient Victorian embodiment of
philistine morality. Inevitably 'Aunt Edna' became the perfect stick for
beating Rattigan's work; even being adopted a decade later by Joe
Orton—under the pseudonym of 'Edna Welthorpe'—as the primary target for the new drama to demolish. (In fact Rattigan clearly struck a
chord here, since she is still with us in the form of Barry Humphrey's
'Dame Edna Everage'.) But the effect of Rattigan's stress on the commercial success of his plays intensified the critical suspicion that he was
selling out his moral, even dramatic principles; and it was this that directly destroyed the very success by which he had justified his work.

Yet the 1950s were the chronological centre of Rattigan's career, his
first play having been staged in 1933 and his last in 1977. Indeed,
throughout the decade, in the face of continuing critical attack as well as
the growing politicization of the theatre from 1956 on, Rattigan dominated the West End. There was hardly a month without at least one of
his plays on the stage; while *Separate Tables* and *Ross* both ran for well
over 700 performances, *The Deep Blue Sea* for more than 500, *Who is
Sylvia?* for 381. By contrast in the early 1960s, as he later recalled: 'I discovered that any play I wrote would get smashed. I just didn't have a
chance with anything.'[7] Rattigan was not exaggerating. *Joie de Vivre*
closed after just four performances in 1960; *Man and Boy* ran for only 69

3.   Terence Rattigan, 'The Play of Ideas', *Theatre Arts*, August 1950, p. 16 (originally published in the *New Statesman and Nation*, 14 March 1950).

4.   Rattigan, 'The Play of Ideas', p. 14

5.   Robert Muller, *Theatre News Letter*, 25 March 1950.

6.   *The Collected Plays of Terence Rattigan* (2 vols.; London: Hamish Hamilton,
1953), II, p. xii

7.   Rattigan, interview in *Kaleidescope*, BBC Radio 4, July 1977.

performances in 1963; and for the next seven years Rattigan withdrew altogether from the stage.

Some 40 years down the road, Rattigan's plays are revived rather more often than Osborne's, or Arden's, and it becomes clear that the critical attack on his work throughout the 1950s had less to do with its actual dramatic quality, than its 'voice'—which Rattigan himself identified as being 'middle-class vernacular'.[8]

But this 'voice', in a rather wider sense, is precisely what makes his plays valuable as documents of the period. It is not so much in the explicit themes of his plays, but in the way these are expressed that Rattigan typifies the Fifties.

To return briefly to Rattigan's self-defeating attack on the 'Play of Ideas': the timing of that essay seems particularly odd since, when it was written in 1950, Osborne was still an obscure actor; Tynan had not yet started on his career; and it would be another three years before Beckett's first play reached the stage. In a sense what Rattigan's essay highlighted was actually the absence of 'ideas' or social commentary in British theatre at the time. The controversy that followed involved James Bridie, Sean O'Casey, Christopher Fry and even Bernard Shaw (in one of his last public utterances). All argued that ideas were inseparable from drama, and that—as when Shaw started writing in the 1890s—there was an urgent need for theatrical renewal. Achieving the opposite of what he apparently intended, Rattigan had created the climate for the founding of the English Stage Company and the emergence of the new playwrights like Osborne and Pinter.

Yet on another level Rattigan, whose essay specifically linked 'ideas' with 'ideology', was serving as a sensitive barometer of the period.[9] In the aftermath of the war against Fascism, this was the height of the Cold War—the Iron Curtain, Stalinism versus MacCarthyism, the outbreak of the Korean war, and the development of the hydrogen bomb: 'ideology', which had almost destroyed Europe in the 1940s, was now threatening the very survival of human society. And though (typically) all this remains an unexpressed subtext in the article, Rattigan can be seen as responding to a widespread fear of social polarization and potentially destructive idealism.

To understand the underlying significance of Rattigan's plays, it is necessary to look briefly at the state of English society in this period. The

8.   *The Collected Plays of Terence Rattigan*, I, p. xix.
9.   Cf. Rattigan, 'The Play of Ideas', p. 15: 'ideology equals intellect'.

Labour government, which came to power as the war ended in 1945, is remembered for the most far-reaching programme of reform that had ever been known in England, in many ways even outdoing Oliver Cromwell. In the six years from 1945 they established the National Health Service and Universal State Welfare; nationalized 20 per cent of British industry and the Bank of England; and committed the economy to full employment through Keynsian techniques. By 1951 all this was in place. The system was set for the 1950s, and beyond. At the same time they pursued the ideal of a classless society through punitive taxation. In this they were extending a process that had already begun under earlier Liberal and even Conservative regimes. Take income tax: in 1913 it had been 8 per cent, in 1919 it was raised to 51 per cent and in 1939 to 78 per cent. Now, from 1945 on, as statements in the House of Commons claimed with pride, the highest incomes were taxed at 94 per cent. Over the same period Death Duties were raised from 15 to 80 per cent.

What this meant in real terms was illustrated by the Labour Chancellor in answer to a parliamentary question in 1950. The very wealthiest citizens, earning £100,000 a year, who would have had £91,700 to spend in 1913, now had an after-tax income of just £2,097. A judge earning £5,000, who would have taken home £4,708 in 1913, was now reduced to £843. Of course, businessmen and professionals in 1950 were paid perhaps five times what their predecessors had earned in 1913; but their real income (not counting for inflation) was still less than a quarter of what it would have been then. As for the judge, whose salary had remained exactly the same over the years: his net earnings were less than 1/6 of his predecessors. The average after-tax pay of the once wealthy middle-classes was estimated to be only 1.8 to 2.6 times the take-home wages of the working class—certainly not enough to sustain their previous life-style.

To bring this down to a personal level, in 1946 Terence Rattigan, by far the highest paid author in Britain, who was stated to earn £600 per week (which works out to £31,200 a year), publicly claimed that he actually had no more than £12 a week to live on—adding up to a meagre £624 in the year.[10] That should be compared to the ceiling below

10. This figure may not be quite honest, since Rattigan was renowned for a lavish life-style, although correspondence from his accountant shows that he was continually in debt. However, it was accepted in the Press without question as being in line with the norm.

which no tax was paid, which was £500 for a family with three children. Thus the childless Rattigan would have had just £2.1s.0d. more a week to spend than a family of workers on minimal wage.

As official figures show, this progressive redistribution of wealth had been taking place over much of the century. Yet it is hardly surprising that (at the time) the whole blame or credit—depending on your point of view—was attributed to the postwar Labour government. And news articles during the 1950s, particularly in American magazines, headlined 'The Destitution of the British Middle Class', or 'The Disappearance of the English Gentleman'.

Since West End audiences were largely middle-class, the public Rattigan aimed at might well be feeling threatened and insecure; and this was reinforced at least into the latter part of the 1950s by a general sense of impoverishment throughout the country. The withdrawal of Marshall Aid at the end of the war together with the sheer cost of the conflict, led to a grim and debilitating austerity, which affected every level of society. At the beginning of the 1950s food was still rationed; reconstruction of the bombed-out cities was slow; and industrial machinery remained unmodernized, unable to compete with a rebuilt Germany.

At the same time, as one commentator noted in 1952: 'the remarkable thing is that on the surface of life there is little visible evidence of the far-reaching levelling of incomes'.[11] Not only were appearances—and social pretensions—still kept up, class accents and attitudes were learnt by the upwardly mobile. So the old hegemony had the appearance, at least, of being completely unchanged. To cap it all, in 1951 the Conservatives were re-elected. Despite the very real social reforms—and the Conservatives, who left the Welfare State as it was, had little choice but to continue the same tax-policies—nothing seemed to have changed in the power-structure (which was indeed Osborne's complaint in *Look Back in Anger*).

In a sense, this sort of double vision was epitomized by the event that opened the decade: the Festival of Britain. Perhaps partly an electoral tool for the Labour government (the 'feel-good' factor), but publicly promoted to offset the climate of austerity and generate new national energy, this celebrated 'Great Britain's contribution to the Arts and Sciences'.[12]

11. J.H. Huizinga, 'The Bloodless Revolution', *Fortnightly*, April–May 1952, p. 258.

12. It is perhaps worth noting note this use of 'Great' that still characterized a

Rattigan himself was commissioned to write a television play for the Festival, *The Final Test*, which was characteristic in combining an innovative technical use of modern media with the most traditional of British sports: cricket. In London, futuristic temporary landmarks—the rocket-shaped Skylon and aluminum bubble of the Dome of Discovery—not only displayed space science and nuclear research, but were inhabited by Shire horses and British cheeses; miniature stages, each set with a scene from Shakespeare accompanied by a snatch of recorded dialogue; and even an 'Eccentricities Section'. Elsewhere (and the Festival was spread over 23 towns and the whole summer from May to the end of September) it was largely, as according to the brochure for Dunster: 'a pageant of knights-in-armour, medieval booths, hucksters, jugglers...monks chanting round the church, minstrels... Morris and country dances, exhibitions of local handicrafts...and a fireworks display'.[13]

In short, what the Festival demonstrated was an almost schizoid state: city-wide illumination at a time of frequent power-cuts; nostalgic illusion versus austerity; the 'Merrie England' of traditional society (as J.B. Priestley admiringly put it) 'at a time when the cost of living is rising steeply and we are bearing a burden of tax that is heavier...than any recorded in history'.[14] And it is precisely this sense of a double life—of an illusory surface disguising a very different, sometimes painful reality—that Rattigan's plays convey.

There are at least three, quite different levels on which we can read any of Rattigan's plays. Take *The Winslow Boy*, first performed in 1946, but revived successfully in 1958 which indicates its continuing relevance to our period. On the level of action it is a courtroom drama about historical injustice. The subtext, specifically relevant for middle-class feelings at the time, showed the triumph of the beleaguered individual in the face of a monolithic state bureaucracy. Such an antagonist could be easily transposed by the audience from the autocratic 1911 Admiralty to the Labour government 35 years later. And indeed that reading was emphasized by Rattigan's comments to the press in advance of the first night, outlining the parallels to the small man's fight for 'ancient free-

Britain agonized over visible impoverishment and the very tangible loss of global power, which effectively sums up this double vision.

13. Advertising brochure, Dunster 1951, np.

14. J.B Priestley, 'The Renewed Dream of a Merrie England', *New York Times Magazine*, 15 July 1951, p. 31.

doms' against 'the new despotism of Whitehall'.[15] However, the play can also be viewed contextually. From this perspective, it is a conscious period piece. Deliberately written in the style of Granville-Barker—the pre-eminent social playwright of the first decade of the century, whose productions of Shaw and Galsworthy were on the stage at the time of the actual events—*The Winslow Boy* was not only appealing stylistically to nostalgia. It indicated the continuance of tradition, with the theatrical form standing for the social attitudes that were becoming increasingly hollow. The imitation also also pointed to Granville-Barker's focus on an inner or 'secret life' (the title of his last play), hidden beneath a surface of social issues.

Rattigan himself repeatedly emphasized the 'power of implication' and the 'weapons of understatement and suggestion' in his plays, claiming that 'drama is inference and inference is drama'.[16] Much of this obliqueness, of course, relates to the homosexual basis of his plays, which—particularly in the 1950s—had to be disguised. Quite apart from 'Aunt Edna's' unwillingness to accept any depiction of homosexuality, which would have led to box-office failure, official censorship was still very much in force. Even the most tacit reference to homosexual preferences would have been banned by the Lord Chamberlain: at least up until the Wolfenden Report in 1957 (which even rated a mention in Rattigan's *Variations on a Theme*). In addition, all homosexual acts, even between consenting adults in private, were illegal. Rattigan himself was living a double life, not only hinting at a possible marriage with Margaret Leighton in the press, but keeping his male lovers strictly segregated from his social life. So it is hardly surprising that both his major plays during the 1950s use heterosexual relationships as disguises for a homosexual original.

In *The Deep Blue Sea*, Hester (who has left her wealthy husband for younger lover and is now being abandoned in her turn) is found lying in front of an unlit gas fire, having tried to commit suicide: the money in the gas meter ran out after she lost consciousness. As Rattigan's biographers have noted, this directly repeats his own tragic experience with a young actor called Ken Morgan who, after living with Rattigan for some years, had walked out on him in 1949 for another man. He then gassed

---

15. Rattigan, 'The Play of Ideas', p. 15. Michael Darlow and Gillian Hodson, *Terence Rattigan: The Man and his Work* (London: Quartet Books, 1979), p. 141.

16. *The Collected Plays of Terence Rattigan*, I, p. xx; 'A Magnificent Pity for Camels', in John Sutro (ed.), *Diversion* (London: Max Parrish, 1950), p. 184

himself in his rented room when that relationship broke up, leaving Rattigan distraught.[17] In fact Rattigan's earliest version of the play had a young man in Hester's role and the lovers were explicitly homosexual.[18]

Similarly, in the first play of *Separate Tables* the histrionic tempestuousness of the alienated lovers echoes Rattigan's own relationships—and in order to get at an emotional reality, some casts have found it helpful to rehearse both characters as men—while in the second play Rattigan himself pointed out that the crime the seedy Major is trying to live down (a conviction for indecently exposing himself to a young woman in a cinema) was originally a homosexual act. In fact, the inspiration for this was Gielgud. Charged in 1953 with a homosexual offence, which was plastered across the pages of the Daily Express immediately before he was due to open in a new play, Gielgud literally faced down the publicity. To Rattigan's open admiration, Gielgud refused to withdraw from the production, appearing on the stage as usual.

But the point is not in fact that these plays, as well as *Variations on a Theme*, are disguised transpositions of a forbidden sexuality. Beneath all that, on the contextual level, it is the double nature of Rattigan's work as such—the surface appearance of normality, and the very different reality underneath—that is significant. It is this split-focus that expresses the experience of the 1950s so well: in theatrical terms, the glamour purveyed by Binkie Beaumont and Cecil Beaton versus the 'kitchen sink' drama of Osborne and Wesker. On one hand the new Welfare State, on the other the widespread sense (particularly on the part of its supposed beneficiaries in the working class) that the hierarchy of inequality was still intact. Conversely, there was the impoverishment of the middle-class versus the appearance of a traditional lifestyle that they still kept up. On the public plane, the glittering lights and traditionalism of the Festival of Britain, followed two years later by the rhetoric of a 'new Elizabethan age' and the pageantry of the Queen's Coronation —for which Rattigan wrote a 'Coronation play', *The Sleeping Prince* (showcasing the reigning couple of the theatre, Laurence Olivier and Vivian Leigh)—versus the bleak postwar austerity, which only began to fade during the 1950s.

Then, too, there was the disintegration of the Empire, the dramatic decline in Britain's global status. Throughout the 1950s, the country still

17. Cf. Darlow and Hodson, *Terrence Rattigan*, pp. 173-75.

18. This script is referred to by Gielgud and others, but does not seem to have survived—it is not with the papers acquired by the British Library.

clung to the illusions and trappings of imperial power—even after the Suez debacle had shown these to be empty posturing. And it is no accident that Rattigan frames the decade with two plays about Empire: *Adventure Story* in 1949, and *Ross* in 1960.

The first dealt with the one historical figure who could be seen to have conquered as far-flung an Empire as Britain in its heyday: Alexander the Great. In drawing a picture of this quintessential empire-builder as man who starts off with democratic ideals, only to end up a tyrant, Rattigan may have had Hitler and Stalin in mind, as his letters show. But being performed barely a year after the loss of India, the 'jewel in the crown', Alexander's key question 'Where did it first go wrong?'[19] echoes what must have been a common British response to the loss of global prestige—while the transience of Alexander's empire, which disintegrated with his death, was all too apt.

Ross, written right at the end of the decade, showed one of the last of the imperial heroes (T.E. Lawrence) as a man hollowed out by his victories, and destroyed by the revelation—under homosexual assault—that he had been driven by unrecognized urges he despised. As at least one of the reviews recognized, Rattigan was presenting 'the uneasy specular symbol of the conscience of the West in the twentieth century. After both the great wars of our time the victorious powers have been assailed by feelings of guilt'.[20] But the obvious analogy was far closer to home...

Osborne and Arden were writing explicitly against the society of their time, demanding a change in the apparent status quo, and in a sense pre-empting that change in the new tone or the stylistic experimentation of their plays. They might, as Ken Tynan claimed, have been speaking for all the young—but the impact of their plays was so powerful, precisely because they were not talking the 'official' language, or expressing normative assumptions.

Rather it is Rattigan who encapsulates the period. Not so much because he identified with 'the Establishment'—even though he certainly did so, writing plays for the Coronation, and at the request of the Duke of Edinburgh, and accepting a knighthood. Not even because he aimed his work specifically at middle-class audiences, and (although to a lesser degree than his critics assumed) pandered to their tastes. But because, beyond any political implications, the deeper structures of his drama voiced the dominant feelings of society as a whole. The doubleness, the

19. *The Collected Plays of Terence Rattigan*, II, p. 107.
20. Harold Hobson, *Sunday Times*, 15 May 1960, p. 25.

split vision, the opposition between a sometimes cliched external experience and an inner, secret life—not just in terms of the characterization,
but contextually—subliminally expresses a social consciousness unique to
the period. It encapsulates the psychology of the 1950s.

Harold Pinter's Recollections of his Career in the 1950s: An Interview Conducted by Ian Smith at the British Library, 1997

Transcribed by Vanessa Toulmin and Dominic Shellard

Ian Smith: Welcome to the British Library, Harold. Would it be fair to say that during the 1950s you were predominantly acting?

Harold Pinter: Yes, I was acting from 1949 actually—although I was not only acting—but that is what I did for a living, certainly. I did quite a lot of it. I started in Ireland with a Shakespearean actor manager Anew McMaster,[1] and then I was with the Donald Wolfit[2]—again Shakespeare, at the King's, Hammersmith in 1953—and then I did a great deal of rep throughout the country. But I was also writing poetry and I also managed to write a novel, so I was active in other respects, too.

IS: From the point of view of the Conference—which has talked about transitions in British theatre in the 1950s and the question of how abrupt or radical those transitions were—it seems remarkable to think that *The Caretaker* stands at the backend of the decade and that in 1950 you were with an actor/manager company playing Shakespeare and you were playing Iago.

HP: Yes, I played Iago and that was with Mac, and I was Bassanio and Horatio and I once did a Hamlet, a matinee (*laughter from the audience*). McMaster played Hamlet and he said, 'I'm tired, do you want to play Hamlet?' and I said 'Absolutely yes', since I was just about 20. I knew

1. 1894–1962. Irish actor manager, who founded his own company to present Shakespeare before the second world war and toured Ireland extensively in the post-war years. Pinter published an appreciation of him, *Mac*, in 1968.

2. 1902–1968. English actor-manager, specializing in Shakespearean and classic roles.

the lines and I knew the whole part without rehearsing it at all, and so I went on and did it and Mac played the gravedigger and he said to me after the show 'Very good dear boy, very good. Next time be kinder to your mother' (*laughter from the audience*) but there never was a next time, I'm afraid.

IS: Did you play any Shakespeare in London?

HP: Yes, I did. I played with Donald Wolfit in 1953 but I had much lesser parts. I played second murderer in *Macbeth* I think and one of the Sals in the *Merchant of Venice* and one or two other odds and sods. I was 9 Knight in *King Lear*. But Wolfit was a great King Lear and I had seen him when I was at school in the 1940s so I was somewhat in awe of him. Consequently, when I was on the stage with him when he was saying 'Oh you unnatural hags' I was so overwhelmed by this experience that I remember I started to cough (*HP coughs repeatedly*) and Wolfit, under his 'Oh you unnatural hags', just glared at me and afterwards his voice rang down the corridors—I remember very well—saying 'Pinter'. 'Yes, sir?' 'You coughed... *Watch it*'. But we didn't really hit it off very well, in fact not at all.

IS: Tell us about the *Merchant of Venice* production with Mac.

HP: Oh yes, well that was another. There was so many...when I was invited to come here and talk about my recollections of the 1950s, I wondered whether I actually had any, you know, I'm not at all sure now what recollections I actually have. There's one vivid little story I can tell you, one theatrical anecdote which is absolutely true. When I was playing Bassanio with McMaster and he was Shylock, I did say to him one night instead of 'for thy three thousand ducats here is six' I actually said 'for thy three thousand buckets here is six' (*laughter from the audience*) and the whole cast actually turned up stage, I remember, apart from McMaster himself, who simply looked at me not batting an eyelid and said 'if every bucket in six thousand buckets'—and it was terribly difficult to carry on (*laughter from the audience*).

IS: Somebody said earlier that in 1954 there were 24 Shakespearean productions in London, possibly even reviewed by a single critic, such as Hobson[3] or Tynan.[4] What do you think the audiences' feelings towards

---

3.   Harold Hobson (1904–1988). Theatre Critic of the *Sunday Times*, 1947–1976. Credited with single-handedly rescuing Pinter's career with his review of *The*

Shakespeare were in those days? Was there a genuine audience of people who were committed to seeing those plays and filling the theatres?

HP: Well, I can't remember 24 Shakespearean productions in London in 1954. I remember when I was with Wolfit at the King's, Hammersmith in 1953 there was a remarkable company just down to the road at the Lyric, Hammersmith with Peter Brook in fact, with Paul Scofield and John Gielgud. They did *Venice Preserv'd* and a number of other remarkable things, I can't remember which they were now. But there were also Jacobean productions earlier. I saw *The White Devil* in London and *The Duchess of Malfi*, I think in 1948 and 1949. Can you imagine such a thing now commercially? This was at the Theatre Royal, Haymarket with Margaret Rawlings and Robert Helpman and so on and it was wonderful to hear that language on the stage. As for audiences, my Shakespearean memories come from Ireland mainly and it really was quite something to play Shakespeare to a whole range of audiences throughout very small halls in small villages in Mayo and Connamara and so on, to little packed houses. These were village halls mostly and that was a remarkable experience certainly. They were very alive audiences and there was a story which went around about McMaster saying that when he came to a town someone said to him 'Ah Mr MacMaster, well you have a lovely company, a lovely company, all the boys is like girls' *(laughter from the audience)*.

IS: Do you think there was a different kind of acting technique to deal with that sort of diversity and perhaps the rough human nature of the theatrical public?

HP: Well, I think we were very bold, you know. The whole thing was very much out front. It's very difficult for me to talk about those kinds of general facts because I was part of it, so I can't really stand outside and make a general observation. I can't analyse the whole thing or even describe it, it was my life and it was a very tough one, too, by the way. I should point out that with McMaster in Ireland, for example, in the early 1950s, we played every night of the week and two matinees. So we played nine performances a week—there was no day of rest whatsoever—and those nine performances were nine different plays. In other

Birthday Party. See Dominic Shellard, *Harold Hobson: Witness and Judge* (Keele University Press, 1995).

4.   Kenneth Tynan (1927–1980). Theatre Critic of the *Observer* 1954 to 1958 and 1960 to 1963, then Dramaturg of the National Theatre.

words we would open with *Othello* on Monday (we travelled by truck incidentally, it was true fit-up), we put up the set, such as it was and got into our tights and on we went and did *Macbeth* or *Othello*, then *The Merchant of Venice* and then a matinee of *As You Like It*, *Oedipus Rex* in the evening, then Mac would have a night off and we did *The Importance of Being Earnest* and we went on like that and on Saturday night we played *King Lear* and then went on to the next town. We were playing in the next, in Limerick as it were, on the Sunday night, the next day.

IS: How much rehearsal did you have before you went on the road with this stuff?

HP: I think we had two weeks rehearsal for nine plays *(laughter from the audience)*. But the point was you had to know all the parts, you would be dead letter perfect from the word go, but it was a very young company apart from himself.

IS: What sort of direction did he give you?

HP: Oh, just speak up, get on with it, *(laughter from the audience)* 'Can't hear a word you're saying, dear boy'—it was that.

IS: As a technician, were you conscious of any change in acting technique over the decade? I've heard it said that the British tradition of voice orientated acting came to be, if not challenged, then certainly affected by continental and American thinking about acting in the 1950s.

HP: Well, again, I can't say whether I did or I didn't, you know I don't think in those terms, I'm not a theorist, I leave it to you to write essays. I repeat, I was simply part of it and I can't now look back and say there was a distinction between one kind of acting and another. I do know of the idea of there being two important elements, crucial elements. One was clarity of diction and the other was truth, and artificiality was not encouraged and posturing wasn't encouraged either. This was out there in Ireland. Wolfit didn't do that either. Although he was regarded by some as flamboyant and unreal, he didn't regard himself as such at all. He believed that he was actually expressing the true image of Shakespeare. He thought he was being totally faithful to the actual image and that he was articulating what Shakespeare intended—and in many respects he was absolutely right.

IS: And from that you had the period in Rep that you mentioned.

HP: Yes, I was going to tell you about when I left Wolfit in 1953. I found myself, I think it was about 1954, in Whitby in Yorkshire in a summer season and I got the job as the leading man up there. The company was run by a man called Lorraine, I remember his name very well, he was a butcher actually, a wealthy butcher, and this was his hobby really, running the summer season. And I formed a very close friendship with an ASM called Rosemary and Rosemary and I used to walk by the beach. Whitby is on the sea I remind any of you who don't know this. We used to walk along the beach after the show at night in the moonlight and it was a very happy couple of weeks. We didn't just walk, we stopped too, in fact! One night I was on stage, acting in something or other, and I saw Rosemary standing in the wings in tears, and I was mystified by this. When I got off the stage, I went over and said 'What in heaven's name is the matter' and she said 'I've been sacked and I've been given two weeks money in lieu of notice'. I said 'What on earth for?' and she said 'Immorality' and in fact that was the case: she had been sacked because her landlady had noticed that she was coming back late from not so much the show but from the beach at night and she told Mr Lorraine and Mr Lorraine just sacked her like that. This was about, as I say, 1954, perhaps even 1955, and so I called Mr Lorraine that night and said 'I gather you've given Rosemary the sack' and I said 'This is very unfair, can you reconsider your decision?'. He replied 'Don't talk to me like that, you just get on with it and you watch your step in future', so I said 'Well, I'll watch my step in future but the fact is that this is a very unjust thing and I don't think you can do that'. He said 'She's a whore and she's going and that's that', so I said 'I think that's a harsh description' (*laughter from the audience*) and I said 'Anyway, what about me?'. He said 'You just watch your step and don't do it again'. So I said 'No, that's not really good enough, Mr Lorraine. We'll be more discreet in the future, shall we say that and we won't walk along the beach too late at night and so on and so on' but he said 'No, no, no, no threats from you, now don't try to blackmail me'. So I said 'No, actually Mr Lorraine, if she goes, I go' and he said 'What?' and I said 'Yes, that is the case' and then he bawled and shouted and screamed and so on and so on and said that I'd be blackballed for ever throughout the whole of the theatre and never work again—but it didn't quite work out like that.

But there were two complications: one was that this girl, Rosemary, had her fiancee in Huddersfield and the second complication was that Bill Gaskill,[5] who I heard mentioned earlier, was there as the Stage

5.   English theatre director, born 1930.

Director, which was a kind of Stage Manager, and doing his first production ever at Whitby. I was rehearsing it, you see, and I called him and said 'I'm off in the morning' and he said 'You can't, you're playing the leading part in my first production' and I said ' I have to go'. And I did go and I got on the train the next morning with no money at all and was met by the police at Euston and went back to my mother who paid the bill, paid the train fare. But my point in telling that story, if there is a point, I think there is one, is that it was a very, very restrictive period really. You mentioned the Lord Chamberlain earlier and he was very much in action, very powerful and there were these constraints on behaviour, you had indeed to watch your step all over the place. It was really in some respects, a very, very grey period.

IS: Did you feel that about British life generally? I've read reminiscences of yours about war time and, in many ways, you've said that was quite a stimulating period of time because of the intensity of experience of life.

HP: During the war, yes, but I think that in the late 1940s and early 1950s it was much bleaker, it became really quite bleak. You see there was also the Cold War, which really got off the ground and I think a lot of us were very conscious of that, I certainly was, because I was a conscientious objector about 1948 and refused National Service. I nearly went to prison twice, but they fined me twice instead. You had to conform, there was a great, great deal of conformity about. We were also very conscious in the early 1950s (in the time you are talking about) of the McCarthy trials in America and the horror of that and I think my detestation of the manifestations of American power probably began or was solidified then. Because, although we had no television, we did have a lot of radio and we also had the British MovieTone News. When you went to the cinema you saw about a 15 minute news programme and I always remember this chap, whatever his name was, it wasn't McCarthy but it was someone else, the Chairman of the McCarthy Committee, saying 'Are you or have you ever been a member of the Communist Party?' and then the chap would say 'I moved from Chicago to New York in 1930 and my mother...' and he would interrupt and say 'Answer the question, answer the question, answer the question' (*Pinter mimics the thumping of the table*) and that was the real mark of it. There was a tremendous amount of that going around and we were also very conscious of the bomb, the bomb was at the centre of our consciousness. Now the bomb seems curiously, perhaps even slightly remote, except there is much more of it these days than there was then, I mean infinitely. People actually tend to forget that it exists which I find very curious because I was actually brought up with the bomb; Hiroshima and Nagasaki remain very vivid in my mind and have never gone away.

IS: Did you feel that aesthetics could make a difference?

HP: Aesthetics?

IS: Yes, I know that you had groups of friends around you who were intensely committed to thinking about innovative and progressive aesthetic practice and also to writers like Webster and so on—how did that relate?

HP: Oh, I think you're quite right, that was very much a redeeming feature, in fact there was a contradiction: on the one hand, one was somewhat deeply intimidated and alarmed and depressed by the world around one, and by the power in that world and the illegitimacy somehow of that power. On the other hand, we were really excited and moved and illuminated by art, there was no question about that. A great friend of mine Henry Woolf (who is, I'm very happy to say, in this auditorium tonight) and I were together then, we came from school and we were very close and remain so. In the 1950s, I'm sure he would agree, Shakespeare was a tremendous stimulus to us, in fact Shakespeare dominated our lives to a great extent. We were also were very much on the lookout for new writings and excited by this. I remember Sartre left a great impression, as did Kafka. I was myself very moved and taken with Hemingway and Joyce, but of course in the very early 1950s I suddenly came across Beckett, and that was a real eye opener to me.

IS: Did you come across Beckett's prose first?

HP: Yes, oh yes. I came across an extract from *Watt* in an Irish magazine called *Irish Writing*, in fact. And that's when I got back to London about 1953, I think, or 1952 and I went to the Westminster Library and asked for other books of Beckett and they'd never heard of him. Finally I tracked him down—quite doggedly actually—to the Bermondsey Public Reserve Library and in Bermondsey they had a copy of *Murphy*. So I asked for this copy and it came out and I noticed at the beginning of the book that it had last been borrowed in 1938. So I decided that since nobody else wanted it, I would take it and I still have it, my one criminal act as far as I know. And I showed it to Mr Beckett himself once when he was over here and he was very pleased to see it.

IS: What about *Godot*? Did you see the first production?

HP: Yes, but I also read his books. I immediately got hold of as much as I could and I read *Molloy* and *Malone Dies* and then saw *Godot* I think in 1955, which I loved.

IS: What was so good about it in that context?

HP: Well, for me, it wasn't so much what was good about it, it was the fact it was just a revolutionary piece of work. I have often felt that although I admire a great deal about John Osborne and I thought he was a writer of great energy and I also was very fond of him personally (but that was much later on), I never quite understood the definition or the description of John Osborne as revolutionary writer, you know, part of a revolution in the English theatre, because I thought that that really should apply to Beckett. I mean Beckett was writing originally in French, but that wasn't the point, the point was this was dramatic literature and it was different, it had never been, what Beckett was doing had never been done before, as simple as that. Whereas I think Osborne, not that I am really comparing the two, it's rather silly, but Osborne was basically a naturalistic writer it seemed to me. I thought *Look Back in Anger* was a perfectly good naturalistic play.

IS: Some people compare Osborne to Rattigan—against the grain of this sort of habitual definition of Osborne that you've been talking about —and I note from David T. Thompson's excellent account of your acting career that you had a lead part in *Separate Tables*.

HP: Yes, I played *Separate Tables* in rep.

IS: How did you like that?

HP: Very good part, yes.

IS: And then you were Cliff in *Look Back in Anger*, an acclaimed Cliff.

HP: No, I wasn't acclaimed (*laughter from the audience*). No, I don't remember being acclaimed. I played Cliff in Palmers Green actually, and it's a long way to go to play Cliff. No, I must tell you that when I was doing *Separate Tables*, that was at Torquay so it wasn't a matter of being acclaimed anywhere really, one just got on with one's job... But I must remind you that although I talked about working hard with McMaster in Ireland, it was really nothing to working in a weekly rep in England. We rehearsed, we opened a play on Monday, started to rehearse the next play on Tuesday morning, started to learn the lines of the next play on Tuesday afternoon, went on with the same play that you were doing on Tuesday night, rehearsed Wednesday morning, matinee and two performances on Wednesday, etc etc, runs through on Friday, and two performances on Saturday and then you were on on Monday. So it was tremendously hard work, very very demanding indeed, but as a matter of fact, while I was doing *Separate Tables* in Torquay, in fact, my friend Henry Woolf, the same Henry Woolf who was at Bristol University and was part of the new Drama Department, rang me and reminded me that I had said to him that I might write a play at some point. I'd just said this in passing a few months before, and I said 'Well I might, I might, but it's going to take me months and months and months'. So he said, 'It can't take you months and months because in a couple of weeks I've got a slot in this Drama Department and I need it, I need your play'. So I said, 'You're crazy, I can't possibly write a play just like that' and he said 'Just think about it for goodness sake, I need it'. So I went back and in fact I then wrote my first play, *The Room* in four days, mostly in the afternoons between rehearsal of one play and the performance of *Separate Tables* in the evening, and then late at night. And then Henry did the play, which was quite an experience, really. I happened to go down there, and I couldn't see it because I was working normally, so I went down on a Sunday and they gave a special performance, I recall, and I was so overwhelmed by the experience of seeing a play of my own on the stage—since it had never happened to me before—that I got totally drunk and I think made a terrible fool of myself one way or the other. But it remains a memorable and unforgettable experience.

IS: When was the next time you saw your work on stage?

HP: Well, the next time was when I saw *The Birthday Party*, which was a total disaster in London in 1958. By that time I was working at the Royal Court, I was an understudy there with Bill Gaskill who'd escaped from Whitby by that time and I understudied actually in a John Osborne play, *Epitaph for George Dillon*, with Robert Stephens.

IS: Did you have a sense that you were changing the face of British drama?

HP: No, not at all (*laughs*)

IS: Or even any aspect of it at all?

HP: No, not in the least. My play *The Birthday Party* was absolutely slaughtered by the critics and there's an interesting story about Kenneth Tynan here. It was quite an event because the play was truly massacred in the month of April/May in 1958 by every single critic apart from Harold Hobson who had liked it, but his review didn't appear until the Sunday. One other critic who could have had some influence on it, on the fate of the play, was, naturally, Kenneth Tynan, and people called him—not me—and he said 'No, he didn't like it very much'. So that's fair enough, he didn't have to and in fact the play closed on the Saturday having run for eight performances. Hobson did come out on Sunday very warmly which meant a great deal to me, I must say, but Tynan was extremely lukewarm, it didn't seem to mean very much to him.

But then about, about five or six years later, I was engaged in a television recording about Donald Wolfit actually, a discussion about him, and Tynan was on this programme, in fact he was running it, I think. And he and I found ourselves having a drink in the public bar after the recording. So we had a couple of drinks and he said to me, I assure you this is what he said, he said 'You know Harold, I didn't realise you were such a sort of pleasant fellow, I really had no idea', and I said 'Didn't you?' and he said 'If I'd known that I think I would have taken a very different view of *The Birthday Party*' (*laughter from the audience*). I've been trying to unravel those words ever since.

IS: Were critics what made or broke a play in that day, more or less than they do now, do you think?

HP: Well I suppose they do, yes.

IS: So you do your play now and then you look for the notices with trepidation.

HP: No, I don't look with trepidation any more. No, in fact, I never looked with trepidation. What happened to me then was good for me because no playwright could ever have had a worst start. I mean to be reviled in the way *Birthday Party* was, was very useful really because it just toughened me up, you know. Well, I thought for a moment of giving up writing for the theatre altogether, but then decided not to. The BBC Radio came to my aid actually, but as I say once you've had a reception like this, other receptions pale and it's of no moment, really. I don't expect, I have no expectations now at all, I haven't had critical expectations for 50 years really (*laughter from the audience*).

IS: Well that's cleared that up. About the BBC, again there's been talk today about the extent to which drama began to receive help from the BBC and also the Arts Council at that time. As a working actor and playwright were you conscious of that sort of thing affecting the climate that you were working in?

HP: You mean help from the public…

IS: Yes, public subsidy.

HP: Oh yes, well you see at that time the BBC was something unrecognizable. This also applied to radio as well, with *The Third Programme.* In those days our habits were unrecognizable and we actually used to go— Henry will remember this too—a few of us would go to a very bare room in somebody's digs or lodging house late at night and switch on *The Third Programme* and listen to Pat McGee reading Beckett. And later on, in the early 1960s I should think, drama was something that one absolutely [watched]. People made appointments to go and see something on television. Sometimes they'd say 'No I can't, I can't do this, if I meet you for a drink, or have something to eat, I've got to go back at 9.00 o'clock and watch something that's on the television'. Which is more or less unheard of now, because everyone records everything. But in those days, television was an amazing phenomenon, in the early 1950s, 1960s.

IS: Did you gain as a writer from that diversity?

HP: Well I'm sure I did. Later on, well again in the early 1960s, I started to write films too, so that was later. I've always been as a writer simply possessed of quite a considerable relish for the act of writing, so anything that came my way I grasped and it's been the springboard of my life.

IS: Which writers of verse drama did you admire in the 1950s?

HP: I was a great admirer of Eliot, I mean Eliot meant a great deal to me all the way through, but I also loved Yeats. Incidentally, Yeats had a great impact on me from the point of view of verse drama, I think *Purgatory* is one of the, remains one of the most extraordinary pieces of work. I still think *The Family Reunion* is wonderful, too, but I never myself tried to write verse drama. I was also very amused and entertained by Christopher Fry in those early days, I enjoyed his joie de vivre. Really, great, great skill, I think much underrated. But you see, it seems to be again coming to Beckett, that Beckett, without writing verse drama, which he clearly didn't, because of his natural rhythm if you like,

Beckett can't write ungainly sentences and that is something that is absolutely at the core of his work, a feeling for balance and the structure of sentences. So that I would say was poetic, or is poetic, but I'd never considered writing what you term verse drama.

IS: You might say that the bottom dropped out of that market...

HP: Yes, I suppose so. Eliot somewhere along the line dropped the ball. The ball that he dropped was the one he didn't pick up from *The Waste Land*. I mean in *The Waste Land* he was able to do anything in terms of various kinds of speech, modes of speech, he wasn't anyway restricted. But I think Eliot finally fell upon a very thin line in his later verse dramas, a thin grey line really and remained restricted to a certain upper middle class delivery and that I think was a pity because I didn't think he needed to do that at all really.

IS: Again were you conscious of feeling that there was a theatrical tradition or establishment which was associated with certain classes and social relations and expectations of audiences?

HP: Oh I was, yes, of course, yes. I mean there was a great reluctance on the part of the general audience to depart from what they'd known, known structures of theatre. I'd got this very firmly, don't forget, in Rep when I was working in places like Bournemouth and Eastbourne and so on. They didn't want anything else, they were perfectly happy to go, as it were, and put their feet up. That was what the theatre was normally about, going and putting your feet up and just receive something, received ideas of what Drama was, going through various procedures which were known to the audience. I think it was becoming a dead area and I must say that I would like to assert that I don't believe that Rattigan, who I see is on the bill here today, was part of that dead end. I think he was a writer of great sensibility and intelligence and perception and I think he was very hard done by by Tynan.

IS: He obviously didn't know what a nice chap he was (*Pinter laughs*).

HP: Yes, he was, too.

IS: Were you ever heckled or booed by audiences?

HP: Yes, definitely heckled in my time and booed, yes.

IS: But specifically?

HP: In Dusseldorf, I was booed in Dusseldorf.

IS: Anywhere in England in those days?

HP: No, unhappily I've never been booed in England (*laughter from the audience*).

IS: Despite your speciality in sinister parts in those days?

HP: No. You mean hissed? (*Pinter laughs*). No, unfortunately not, but life is still young, there is plenty of time.

IS: I get a sense from you that you look back on working in Rep under those, to me, incredible conditions of intensity of work and being forced to memorize all that stuff, you look back on that and, whereas some people would say well later on theatre allowed more space for people to concentrate and develop, you look back on that as a period of incredible vitality and training.

HP: Oh I do absolutely, you really had to get on with it. I directed a play a couple of years ago in London, *Twelve Angry Men*, which was written in fact in the early 1950s by Reginald Rose, I don't know how many people here know it, it takes place in a jury, it's a jury play in New York, it's a great film of course. And this was a play in which there were 12 people on the stage all the time, and the 12 actors and me and the designer had to think about how to choreograph the whole thing. It took a great deal of doing, it was very, very challenging, very complicated and wonderfully stimulating because all of us had to find true skills, theatrical skills, so that all this elaborate choreography and orchestration had to happen without the audience knowing it was happening. The audience had no idea of all the work that had actually gone into this production. But for me it took me back quite a long way to my early days in Rep, but, mind you, I've always been extremely fascinated by movement on stage. In fact, incidentally, the alliance, the fusion between word and movement and stillness and activity and action. It's a continual source of fascination for me, because I think that determines what's happening, it puts the seal on someone. If someone moves (as I was talking about Beckett taking such pains about the rhythm of his sentences) I also think that what you're looking at on stage must possess a shape which is finally definitive, and again the audience may not realise that that's what is happening, that's what you've been striving for, but that is the exercise, that is the thing one is doing all the time. If I move my little finger the wrong time, even in a thousand seat theatre, that will distract and be like something falling off a train, something clattering off a train as it passes under a bridge, you know what I mean? I remember seeing Wolfit, when he waited in *Oedipus Rex*. We were all down stage as the Chorus and he was standing right up on a plinth with an enormous cloak and his son, whatever his name was, I can't remember, made a long speech to him. You couldn't see the son and couldn't see Wolfit either as a matter of fact, because he had his back to the audience. And then finally Wolfit stood up and he waited until the speech was over and did that (*Pinter goes to the rear of the stage, turns his back on the audience, pauses for several seconds and then swoops around*).

I remember when we did *The Homecoming* first, the idea of a glass of water being put down and picked up seemed to me like that cloak going *pssssshhhhh*. It was a moment that was very specific and very precise and fun actually. That's why I find still theatre to be a most exciting activity.

IS: I think that's a nice closing cadence for our interview. Would anybody like to put a question?

Audience Member 1: Do you actually think that we need critics to reinterpret what the writer is trying to say to us and are critics really just those who lack the courage to sit down and produce original work?

HP: I do think that you are asking the wrong man, I do think you should actually ask a critic (*laughter from the audience*).

Audience Member 1: The reason I'm actually asking is because I do actually write critiques and I am beginning to question myself if it's the right thing to do.

HP: Well, I have to say, that although I said a while ago that for 50 years I haven't expected anything from critics at all, that's not entirely true, because when one does receive a perceptive and intelligent review, one is, of course, gratified and there can be meetings of minds you know. They can be understanding of someone's piece of work and that indeed is valuable when that happens. But actually the other side of the coin is equally true, where that is not the case, where you actually simply get a kind of bovinity, which I do think is part of where we are now—but not in this room, I hasten to add. That is grating and irritating and annoying, but what happens finally is that you shrug it off. As for the final value of critics, I honestly can't say, I think on the whole they are a pretty self-serving lot and also pretty ignorant. The one thing that critics absolutely know nothing about is acting, for example. That is the one thing about Tynan, I've said a few words about Tynan just now and I must say that I would like to correct one thing, he really knew what an actor was, what actors were doing and some of his writing on acting is very fine writing, no question about it, superb actually. But generally critics don't know what acting is. What I find more and more in the professional theatre in this country, I am not going to name names here, but I think that...

IS: Go on...

HP: No, no, no I think I'd be booed and hissed, but there are certain female performers in this country who have an extraordinary reputation, shall we say they are stars of a kind, but what they are really doing is simply exhibiting themselves. In my view acting doesn't come into it, it's an exhibition and a parade of various characteristics or mannerisms, I find it just laughable, but it interests me sociologically to see that this is what acting means to so many critics, this is what the word acting means. So finally I find the role of the critic not terribly persuasive.

Audience Member 2: You've talked of shape and structure and form in Beckett's work and it seems to me that your work exhibits similar characteristics. Could we say that this belief in form and structure accounts for the incredible stylistic consistency of your plays from the 1950s, right the way through to now?

HP: Well, it's very difficult for me to make any statement or certainly judgment on my own work, you know, extremely difficult. I do know that I certainly do take great pains to find a structure which is satisfying and harmonious. Something that possesses integrity, if you like. But I don't think in those terms when I'm writing, in fact I don't think at all when I'm writing I simply let it go, so that what happens is there's an odd mixture I think in my own experience of writing extremely fast (which I do when I begin something) and going at it, like I say, without any thought, certainly no thought about structure, it just goes smack into it, like going into a dark tunnel. But finally coming out of the tunnel and looking at what is on the page and without, I hope, taking away the vitality of the actual experience of writing in the first place, shaping it. I often find that some of it, a good deal of it is already shaped, although I didn't know it was. It's shaped itself, but apart from that it's very difficult, as I say, to make any real judgement on my own, the way I work, or what comes out in the end. But I hope you're right (*Pinter laughs*).

Audience Member 2: Are there other people that you particularly admire for form?

HP: There are lots but I can't think of one of them at the moment.

Audience Member 3: My question now comes as a pendent to the last one. You didn't quite beat the record for speed in playwriting, Coward wrote *Private Lives* in three days on a boat, but he made the point that he had been thinking about that play for a considerable time before he picked up pen and paper. In relation to your own work, you also write speedily for your first draft, you're not a comma chaser, if I can put it like that...

HP: Never have been.

Audience Member 3: No. How far have you been thinking, consciously or subconsciously about a play that might pop out, sorry to describe it in that cavalier way?

HP: Well, you know, that's really an impossible question to answer. I do know that my last play, *Ashes to Ashes*, has been on my mind for about over 50 years and it popped out, as you say, the year before last and suddenly I found I was writing it. But I know that actually the content of the play has been on my mind for 50 years. I know so many things hang about in one's mind, they are all there, they go down and come up and then go away and sometimes are lost forever. That's I think one of the sad things that does happen to the human mind and certainly if you are a writer, that you—I am sure it's every writer's experience—you sometimes have a wonderful idea in the middle of the night, can't find a piece of paper or a pen, go to sleep, wake up and have lost it and never find it again. That's a terrible thing that to happen actually, you feel a real gap in your mind, where has it gone and never recount, sometimes never recount it. But other times, the other side of the coin, is that they do crop up and suddenly hit you out of nowhere.

Audience Member 4: My question deals with some names that came up during today, names of people like Rattigan and Tynan. One person that intrigues me is Binkie Beaumont[6] in the 1950s, so many people in the 1950s seem to have been affected by him but there is very little

---

6.   Theatre producer, director of H.M.Tennent Ltd, responsible for many of the West End successes between 1945 and 1960. Treated with suspicion by the writers of the new realist theatre from 1955 onwards.

written about him or known about him and I just wondered if you had a view about him or whether you'd ever met him or really whether you felt he was a benign or a destructive influence on the theatre.

HP: Oh, I met him yes, I did meet him absolutely, he wasn't destructive, I don't see how he can be described as destructive but he wasn't particularly benign either. He was a very sharp man, he had a very quick tongue, he was pretty ruthless, but he had tremendous energy and he, as they say, loved the theatre, he really did and I think he put all his life into it, so he was undeniable as a force. I think he did some remarkably good work, he helped a lot of people and the theatre in Shaftesbury Avenue, let's face it, in so far as it was a living theatre, which it was to a certain extent, was nevertheless flourishing, one has to say that, it really did flourish and he was the centre of it, he put all the money into it, he got the whole thing going really, so you've got to take your hat off to him for that. His horizons were pretty limited and he didn't see very far really, but he did love the theatre and he was okay. There's another anecdote I have about him but it's too obscene to tell I think (*laughter from the audience*).

IS: Surely not, the Lord Chamberlain is not here!

HP: It's nearly six o'clock

IS: There's a man in a white shirt who has had his hand up every time.
Audience Member 5: If we are to move away from a linear plot, can we also move away from a playwright in the theatre and is there any space for a theatre without a playwright?

HP: It seems to be the case now, there's a great deal of theatre which has nothing to do with writers at all, is there not? I mean, in other words, a communal or shared experience, creation by groups of people—more and more and more that is so. I myself am very old fashioned, I remember when I was auditioning an actress, years and years ago and she said 'Can I improvise first?' and I said 'What?' and she said 'Well I like, before I read your play, your speech from your play, I'd like to improvise' and I said 'Okay, you improvise and I'll come back in ten minutes', which I did. So I left and she had a great time improvising. It's not my cup of tea really, in other words. But I can't deny it's happening all the time. To a certain extent if you look at the group activity like Ballet, which suddenly comes to me, of course there's a choreographer. Nevertheless, there's a sense of discovery between actors or dancers which I think is perfectly valid and we do it anyway, that actually happens anyway. Except I believe in the text and I stick to that text, and I think others should, too, in relation to my own work, I mean.

Audience Member 6: Apart from thoroughly enjoying your plays, there's some work you've done in various media, you've taken plays and turned them into radio plays, taken plays and turned them into films, you've taken novels and turned them into plays, can you talk about the way you translate from one medium to another?

HP: Well, I don't know quite what there is to talk about really, I just do it. I enjoy that transposition and I find that different challenges are embodied in whatever medium we're talking about and different questions are asked and different answers are to be found. For example, shortly someone is going to do my play *Old Times* on radio, and that immediately sets up questions of how to do it because the centre of *Old Times* is purely visual, you know it is actually visual, the beginning and the end. So how to solve that question is the question and, in fact, the director is coming round to see me next week and we'll discuss it, whether we find an answer, I really don't know. You can always find an answer but is that answer the correct one? In other words, should we do it at all? These are questions I really don't know, so they all represent different and very specific problems and it's great fun doing it.

IS: Do you have time for one more?

HP: One more.

Audience Member 7: Just about the issue of improvization which came up in the question behind me, I was wondering what you thought of the work of Theatre Workshop in the late 1950s, particularly, and how do you see that relating to your own work: Joan Littlewood, for example.

HP: Well it didn't have any relation to my own work at all really, but I did admire the vitality of the operation and I remember I saw Brendan Behan's *The Hostage* and there was no denying the tremendous juice they had down there. There was a sense of a pioneering activity going on, which was very, very alive. But Joan Litttlewood and I had very little in common really, so we didn't work together or anything like that.

IS: Thank you, Harold, for being such a marvellous interviewee and performer and for giving us such a fascinating set of reminiscences.

Looking Back at *Godot*

John Bull

Over the years there has been little disagreement about both the nature and the precise starting point of the 'new wave' in British drama in the 1950s. John Russell Taylor's 'guide to the new drama', as it was described on the cover when it was first published in 1962, nailed its colours firmly to the mast with its title, *Anger and After*. Taylor makes the point unambiguously in the very first paragraph of the book which is still the first resort for students anxious to acquaint themselves with the period: 'The whole picture of writing in this country has undergone a transformation…and the event which marks 'then' off decisively from 'now' is the first performance of *Look Back in Anger* on 8 May 1956'.[1] Kenneth Tynan, the contemporary theatre's severest critic, made the same claim looking back in 1964: 'It all came to a head one May evening in 1956 at the Royal Court Theatre'.[2] Taylor's and Tynan's location of Osborne's play as the starting-point received a ready consensus from, among others, Alan Carter, the author of an early book on the playwright—'there is no doubt that *Look Back in Anger* was the play which marked the so-called breakthrough in the theatre of post-war Britain'[3]—and, indeed, from the man himself. Offered the chance to write the first commissioned play in the new National Theatre complex, and the opportunity to make history, Osborne refused, allegedly telling Sir Laurence Olivier, 'I've already made expletive history'. The claims for *Look Back in Anger* rapidly became enmeshed with a somewhat mythical account of the original aims and intentions of the English Stage

---

1.   John Russell Taylor, *Anger and After: A Guide to the New British Drama* (Harmondsworth: Pelican, 1962), p. 11.

2.   Kenneth Tynan, *Tynan on Theatre* (Harmondsworth: Penguin Books, 1964), p. 54.

3.   Alan Carter, *John Osborne* (London: Oliver & Boyd, 1969), p. 18.

Company at the Royal Court Theatre where John Osborne's play was first produced. Thus, by 1975, Martin Esslin is able to offer a 'Foreword' to the first published history of the Company—Terry Browne's *Playwright's Theatre* of 1975—in which the play is given precisely the same ground-breaking role:

> the success—or *success de scandale* of Osborne's *Look Back in Anger* revealed...the fact, hitherto unsuspected by the commercial entrepreneurs of the theatre, that plays dealing with lower class characters speaking a non-standard English and flouting the conventions of the 'who's for tennis' school of playwriting could actually become profitable theatrical ventures.[4]

My intention is neither to attempt a revisionist account of the Royal Court experiment, nor yet to deny its supreme importance in the development of the new drama. I want, rather, to first suggest some alternative views on the starting-point of this new drama and, more interestingly, to argue for some connections. On 4 June 1956, *The Times* newspaper reported that *Look Back in Anger* had proved to be so popular that additional performances had been arranged. That same day it also heralded the imminent first visit to England of Bertolt Brecht's Berliner Ensemble, bringing with it productions of *The Caucasian Chalk Circle*, *Mother Courage* and *Trumpets and Drums* (Brecht's adaptation of Farquhar's *The Recruiting Officer*). Interestingly, the terms of reference for welcoming these productions are quite the opposite of those that I quoted making claims for *Look Back in Anger*. Where both Taylor and Esslin had placed the significance of Osborne's play in an essentially local context, as offering theatre audiences the opportunity to discover a hitherto unheard part of English society, *The Times* declared,

> The last place in which to be insular is the theatre, which is seldom so full of ideas that it can afford to disdain inspiration from other lands, so that it is good reason to welcome...the Berliner Ensemble from East Berlin.

That Brecht should be bringing to England two of the three great Epic plays of his mature years (the third being *Galileo*) would have alone made this a significant event, but that it introduced most of the London audiences to a style of theatre and performance quite alien to the native defiantly non-politicized tradition made it momentous. George Devine, the artistic director of the Royal Court, had directed Shakespeare's *King Lear*

4. Martin Esslin, 'Foreword', in Terry Browne, *Playwright's Theatre: The English Stage Company at the Royal Court* (London: Pitman, 1975), pp. iii–iv.

in 1955 as his final commitment before his involvement with the English Stage Company. Between September and December the production was on the road, and one of the stopping-off points was Berlin, where Brecht and Helene Weigel attended a matinee and joined Devine and Peggy Ashcroft for beer and sausages afterwards.[5] Devine later tried to make arrangements for his *enfant terrible* John Osborne to visit East Berlin and work with the Berliner Ensemble, though nothing came of it. However, after *Look Back in Anger* had been given an extended 11-week run, until September 1956, it was only forced off the stage of the Court because Devine had secured Brecht's agreement for him to direct his first work by the playwright, *The Good Woman of Setzuan*,[6] with Ashcroft in the lead-role and Osborne, still partly employed as a actor, as a peasant gardener.[7] Alan Carter is not alone in seeing evidence of the influence of Brecht in the 'epic frame-work of Archie's music-hall turns'[8] in Osborne's next play, *The Entertainer*, which opened at the Royal Court in April 1957. And, certainly, by 1961, it was difficult not to notice the influence when, with *Luther*, Osborne took on a non-English subject for the first time. Not only did the play echo the Epic structure of Brecht's *Galileo*, in particular, but it used the figure of the Knight to introduce the action of each carefully separated scene.

The most important of the next generation of new writers, Edward Bond, has said that the key event to shape his early writing was this visit of the Berliner Ensemble;[9] and, in the 1960s, John Arden said that *Mother Courage* was the play he would most like to have written,[10] many contemporary critics seeing evidence of the influence of Brecht's ideas in both *Serjeant Musgrave's Dance* and *Armstrong's Last Goodnight*. But the strong influence of Brecht was not really to be felt in Britain until the 1970s and the second new-wave of post-1968 playwrights,[11] and was

5. Irving Wardle, *The Theatres of George Devine* (London: Eyre Methuen, 1979), pp. 169-70.

6. Wardle, *The Theatres of George Devine*, pp. 184-85.

7. John Osborne, *Almost a Gentleman* (London: Faber & Faber, 1991), pp. 29-30.

8. Carter, *John Osborne*, p. 32.

9. Malcolm Hay and Philip Roberts, *Bond: A Study of his Plays* (London: Eyre Methuen, 1980), p. 16.

10. Charles Marowitz and Simon Trussler, *Theatre at Work* (London: Eyre Methuen, 1967), p. 47.

11 Cf. John Bull, *Stage Right: Crisis and Recovery in British Contemporary Mainstream Theatre* (Basingstoke: Macmillan, 1994), pp. 42-45.

initially largely confined to details of staging in productions of already extant texts, as in the case of the Royal Shakespeare Company's 'War of the Roses' cycle of Shakespeare's Histories. So, Osborne's superficial borrowings should alert us to the profoundly unBrechtian nature of, even, *Luther*. Bamber Gascoigne made the point well in a contemporary review of the play: 'no analysis of the causes of the Reformation... merely one man's rebellion against the world into which he was born'.[12] But, although Osborne's Luther is, indeed, conceived of primarily in psychologically rather than socially-determined ways, it is already possible to make connections between two different, and ideologically opposed, starting-points for the new drama. There are others.

This was the first time that Brecht had brought his company to England, but his work had been known about in some circles since the 1930s. Joan Littlewood recalls that, when she first met Jimmie Miller (Ewen McColl) he had 'the only typed copies of Brecht's early plays, in German...twenty years before Ken Tynan discovered Brecht for the readers of the *Observer*'.[13] It was McColl who first introduced her to 'agit-prop' theatre and, as early as 1935, their Theatre of Action (a precursor of Theatre Workshop) performed scenes from Brecht's *Puntila and his Servant Matti* and *Roundheads and Peakheads*,[14] though Littlewood continued to be less than 'thrilled' with his work, believing in 1947 that 'in *Mutter Courage* his admired heroine is nothing but a cheap jack, profiting from the country's war',[15] incidentally reacting exactly as Brecht had tried so hard to get his audiences to do towards the character. And then, at the Devon Festival in 1950, Littlewood directed and belatedly agreed to play the lead role in the first staged production of *Mother Courage* in Britain.[16] By 1953 Theatre Workshop had found a home at the Theatre Royal, and it could be argued that this might be as good a place to locate the beginning of the new wave as any of the others so far posited. Certainly, there are links to be made, if not directly with Brecht, then, with the tradition of politicized theatre from which his work emerged. But equally, there are distinctions to be made. The

12. *The Spectator*, 4 August 1961.

13. Joan Littlewood, *Joan's Book: Joan Littlewood's Peculiar History As She Tells It* (London: Minerva, 1995), p. 89.

14. Margaret Eddershaw, *Performing Brecht: Forty Years of British Performances* (London: Routledge, 1996), p. 43.

15. Littlewood, *Joan's Book*, p. 287.

16. C.f. Bull, *Stage Right*, pp. 42-43.

company under Littlewood slowly evolved a solid body of work in which the classics were increasingly mixed with new plays that sought to present a radical and proletarian alternative not only to the traditional mainstream but towards what has been traditionally taken as its chief contemporary opposition, the work of the Royal Court. 'Too soft-centred—very middle-class and proper', as Littlewood described it when, in 1958, the Court had not acknowledged her challenging introduction into a performance of Brendan Behan's *The Hostage* of two dustbins labelled 'Return to the Royal Court', where Samuel Beckett's *Endgame* was currently being staged.[17]

Endgame, produced in tandem with *Act Without Words*, was the first Beckett to be performed at the Royal Court. That the plays were performed in French would have, presumably, only added to the fervour of Littlewood's sneer at the studiedly non-proletarian nature of the enterprise. But this was not the first opportunity British audiences had had to see the work of Beckett. Peter Hall had directed *Waiting for Godot* at the Arts Theatre in 1955, a production that had generated sufficient interest that it was able to transfer to the commercial theatre, an event then without precedent for an avant-garde play. It was, indeed, precisely its commercial success that allowed its producer, Donald Albery of Donmar Productions, to argue in 1960 for a very different starting-point for the 'new wave':

> I always maintain that *Waiting for Godot* was unquestionably the start of the new wave, better than anything since. It was the first stirring of something new and its nine-month run at the Criterion was unheard of in those days for that sort of thing, not a thriller, or a drawing-room comedy or the revival of a classic.[18]

In 1958, Laurence Olivier broke new ground in his career when he agreed to take the role of Archie Rice in Osborne's *The Entertainer*, the production that followed Beckett's double-bill at the Royal Court. In 1960, he was back at the Court again, this time appearing in Eugene Ionesco's *Rhinoceros*, a play that, like *Waiting for Godot*, proved so successful that it too transferred to the commercial theatre for an extended run. Two years earlier Tynan and Ionesco had had their famous disagreement via the pages of *The Guardian* newspaper, Tynan seeking to challenge Ionesco's claims for an essentially non-politicized theatre.

17. Littlewood, *Joan's Book*, p. 538.
18. Quoted in *The Times*, 26 March 1961.

Ionesco was firm in his dismissal of the foregrounding of ideological concerns in the theatre, something that he correctly saw as being central to Brecht's work:

> A work of art has nothing to do with doctrines... A work of art is only ideological, and nothing else, is useless, tautological, inferior to the doctrine which it expresses... An ideological play is nothing more than the vulgarisation of an ideology. In my opinion, a work of art has a system of its own, its own means of direct apprehension of reality.[19]

It was a point he made even more forcefully in his *The Physician's Panorama* of 1963:

> If the theatre is to be relevant today, it has to be a witness...of our spiritual disintegration, by a language that is disintegrated, by situations that are in themselves disintegrated... Social reality is that of unauthentic, two-dimensional hollow man. The theatre must turn its attention inwards.[20]

The echo of the title of T.S. Eliot's 'The Hollow Men' of 1925, and Ionesco's claim for 'spiritual disintegration' as the 'social reality' of the modern world offer precise markers of that sense of futility, of despair, of the powerlessness of the individual in a world in which nothing remained in which to believe, that came to be seen as central motifs of the Absurdist school as it became increasingly defined. And, in this context, the first production of *Waiting for Godot* is correctly recognized as a key moment. Beckett's title was drawn from Simone Weil's *Attente en Dieu* (*Waiting on God*, as it was rendered in the first English translation in 1951); and while, the symbolic structure of Beckett's play allows for a far wider appropriation of what the Godot who is being waited for might represent, it is impossible—especially given the wealth of theological debate within the play—not to accept that one of his manifestations must be God; and that, therefore, Beckett's play is, among other things, an account of the spiritual disintegration attendant upon the losing of that certain knowledge of a God who might give shape to the lives of individuals and societies. Will Godot come, shall we wait? Does Godot exist, shall we go? And in which case, where?

---

19. Eugène Ionesco, 'Le Rôle du Dramaturge', *Notes et Contre-Notes* (Paris: Gallimard, 1962), p. 72. Published originally in Donald Watson's translation in *The Observer*, 29 June 1958. I quote Julian Wulbern's translation in his *Brecht and Ionesco: Commitment in Context* (Urbana: University of Illinois Press, 1971), p. 13.

20. Quoted in *The Times*, 11 February 1963.

David Bradby has talked of the play's characters as having no 'charac-ter'. 'They come from nowhere, have nowhere to go, and are sustained only by a hope that is shown to be at best a comforting illusion, at worst a cruel deception'.[21] However, we can qualify this a little. Beckett's characters do have imperfectly remembered flashes of their past history. In Act I Estragon gets Vladimir to recall the time, perhaps 50 years ear-lier, when they were grape-picking and he threw himself in the Rhone; although when, in Act II, Vladimir attempts to contrast their current scenic location with that of the Macon country where they once picked grapes, Estragon denies having any such memory. We are at least able to place the characters in France, and a France, furthermore, which has other locations to visit, if only to the unseen hay-loft where the boy who brings the message that Mr Godot will not be coming sleeps with his brother. Now, I am not attempting to translate Beckett's play into a piece of social naturalism. Simply to argue that it does have potential socially located roots that have not always been recognized in the many attempts to make sense of the play. The context is postwar Europe, as surely as it is a world of post-nuclear destruction in many of his later plays, from *Endgame* on.

No such problems occur when we turn back to *Look Back in Anger*, as is quickly revealed when we compare the two playwrights' published directions for the stage sets:

Look Back in Anger

> The Porters' one-room flat in a large Midland town. Early Evening. April. The scene is a fairly large attic room, at the top of a large Victorian house. The ceiling slopes down quite sharply from L. to R. Down R. are two small low windows. In front of these is a dark oak dressing table. Most of the furniture is simple, and rather old. Up R. is a double bed, running the length of most of the back wall, the rest of which is taken up with a shelf of books. Down R. below the bed is a heavy chest of drawers, covered with books, neckties and odds and ends, including a large, tattered toy teddy bear and soft, woolly squirrel.

And so on, the close details of the set being followed by even more pre-cise sketches of the play's characters.

21. David Bradby, *Modern French Drama* 1940–90 (Cambridge: Cambridge Uni-versity Press, 1990), p. 59.

Waiting for Godot

> A country road. A tree. Evening.

Although we may infer that Beckett's play is also set in or around April, given that the only change indicated in the stage directions for Act II is that four or five leaves have grown on the tree, the location is deliberately about as imprecise as it could be. In contrast, Osborne gives a very detailed account of the set in ways that offer a conscious opposition to the world of the 'drawing-room' dramas that it is said to have opposed. However, the construction of a set that challenged the established pattern notwithstanding, *Look Back in Anger* looks very conventional in format when put alongside *Godot*. It may have excited, or indeed disturbed, audiences with its articulation of a previously unheard class protest, but it did so in ways that demonstrated how well Osborne had learnt from his apprenticeship as an actor in the old school. But there is more than one way of reading the narrative structure of the play.

No-one, I think, has claimed that Osborne was influenced by Beckett in writing *Look Back in Anger*—and I do not intend to initiate such a move. But examination of the structure of *Waiting for Godot* does reveal some striking similarities to that of Osborne's play. In the structuring of the dialogues involving Vladimir and Estragon and Jimmy and Cliff their creators borrow heavily from a popular culture of, respectively, the circus and the music-hall, the latter of which Osborne was to mourn the passing in his next play, *The Entertainer*. Indeed, the specifically comic elements of both plays depend almost entirely on the appropriation of slapstick and patter routines, one of the features that has historically allowed *Godot* to be embraced into the mainstream theatre. But there are more important parallels to be drawn.

If, as Vivian Mercier memorably claimed, in *Godot* 'nothing happens twice', then in *Look Back in Anger* nothing can be said to happen three times. If *Godot* has a second act that mirrors the actions of the first, both in the narrative thread and in the avoidance of a formal closure to that narrative, it can also be argued that *Look Back in Anger* has a comparably unresolved structure. Jimmy moves from Alison, to Helena and back to Alison—the parallel emphasized by having the two women proclaim their status in Jimmy's world by their occupation of the same ironing-board at the openings of Acts I and III. As in Vladimir and Estragon's two meetings with Lucky and Pozzo, so with Jimmy's alliances with the two women, everything is altered but nothing is changed. Two plays which are so clearly different in style and in the theatrical traditions from which they draw, nonetheless share a comparably circular action in which nothing changes, nothing can be done, and in which the articulation of boredom becomes the most meaningful activity of the day. In both cases, the characters are isolated from an outside world, Beckett's waiting for something that will not happen, and Osborne's Jimmy Porter for something that possibly already has. That Osborne's characters should do so in a naturalistically realised urban dwelling whilst Beckett's do so on an ill-defined French country road leading to and from nowhere should not blind us to the fact that the two writers share a rhetoric of despair that leaves both plays unresolved other than in a general consensus to continue, to survive. For what else is there? For Jimmy, no 'great causes', and for Vladimir and Estragon no Godot.

The connection that I am arguing for is an important one, for it brings with it a very real ideological payload. When it was said that nothing happens twice in *Godot*, the inference is that not only is there a pattern of repetition—Vladimir and Estragon whiling away the time, meeting up twice with Lucky and Pozzo in episodes that declare that nothing is to be hoped for in spiritual, in philosophical or in political programmes, the pair again being disappointed by the non-arrival of Godot—but that nothing either changes or, indeed, can change. The agnosticism of Beckett's play is mirrored in Osborne's. All three acts of *Look Back in Anger* open, not at all coincidentally, on a Sunday, precisely so that the articulation of the boredom of an English Sunday with nothing to do (shades of *Hancock's Half Hour*) can be directly associated with a hostility towards its Christian significance—allowing Jimmy a diatribe against the church bells that announce a Christian service he will not attend in Act I, and an even more sustained outburst in Act II against Helena and Alison after the former has announced, 'She's going to church'.

What *Look Back in Anger* shares with *Godot* is, then, a depiction of a world in which nothing remains in which to believe. It is in stark opposition to Brecht's formulation of a theatre in which he argued that man is 'alterable and able to alter'[22]—that there is, therefore, a continuation of the political narrative of the play that involves its audience after it has left the theatre. The circularity of the absurdist model denies both the intent or the possibility of such a continuation of the dialogue. *Godot* ends with Vladimir asking 'Well? Shall we go?' and Estragon responding

22. Bertolt Brecht, 'The Modern Theatre is the Epic Theatre', in John Willett (ed.), *Brecht on Theatre* (London: Eyre Methuen, 1978), p. 37

'Yes, let's go', and the final stage direction is 'They do not move'. Similarly, Osborne's play ends with Jimmy and Alison reunited in a moment of domestic whimsy, but gives no promise of anything other than a circular movement in the narrative. It was in this manner that Tom Stoppard's *Rosencrantz and Guildenstern*—which, of course took *Godot* as its ur-text—originally concluded, with the names of two attendant lords being called out, and the whole process presumably being about to be set in motion once again.[23]

Mention of Stoppard's play reinforces the strength of the argument for starting with *Godot* because its use of Beckett's text in a production that established the English playwright as a major figure virtually overnight is indicative of the way in which the strands of Absurdism that can be traced back to *Godot*, as well as to Ionesco, had taken over as the model of British avantgarde theatre. What I am saying is that it may have been the sense of contemporaneous naturalism that brought Osborne's play to public notice—particularly once it was appropriated into the new wave of British naturalism in the cinema—but that what made it most 'of its time' was the way in which it paralleled the unprogressive model of which *Godot* came historically to be the dominant embodiment.

A little historical contextualization is in order. If *Look Back in Anger* was the play of the year in 1956, then there is little doubt that the book of the year, in terms of its timeliness and its influence, was Colin Wilson's *The Outsider*. Its popularizing introduction to the outsider figures placed them firmly in the same arena of existentialist doubt that had given rise to Beckett's Vladimir and Estagon. In British terms, it was one of the key texts in the coining of the term 'Angry Young Men' to describe Osborne and others, most notably young novelists. That it should have been published in 1956 now seems almost inevitable. Comparing the two years 1953, the year of the coronation of Elizabeth II, and 1956, Stephen Lacey has written: 'if 1953 was a moment when a traditionalist hegemony and the consensus seemed at its most secure, 1956 saw the hegemonic project begin to falter'.[24] Most importantly, 1956 was the year of the Suez fiasco—a proclamation of the demise of Britain as a

23. The scene was included in the first published edition of the play (London: Faber & Faber, 1968), but is not included the altered text published since the second edition in 1968.

24. Stephen Lacey, *British Realist Theatre: The New Wave in its Context 1956–65* (London: Routledge, 1995), p. 14.

colonial nation—and it was the year of the Russian invasion of Hungary, and the final blow to what remained of a leftist belief that State Communism might provide a way forward. Both these events figure as a subtext in the new wave plays of 1956 and immediately after and, ideologically exciting though the spectacle of the Berliner Ensemble might have seemed, a progressive model of political theatre had as little appeal to the new wave as it had always had to the mainstream.

A further example is inevitable, for between Beckett and Stoppard, stands the figure of Harold Pinter. The contrast between Pinter's first London production and Stoppard's could not be greater. *The Birthday Party* limped out of the Lyric Hammersmith in May 1958 virtually unseen. What critical attention it received placed it confidently as an English version of the Theatre of the Absurd—*The Times*, for instance, talked of it as an 'essay in surrealistic drama...[that] gives the impression of deriving from an Ionesco play which Mr Ionesco has not yet written',[25] a theme repeated in the same newspaper's review of the 1959 Royal Court double-bill of *The Dumb Waiter* and *The Room*—'What can already be applauded are his successes in finding minutely observed English personages to fill a structural framework borrowed from the continental avant-garde'.[26]

Now, what is most interesting about this is Harold Pinter's response. Told in 1960 that *The Birthday Party* owed much to Ionesco, he expressed great surprise—'when I wrote it... I had only seen one of his plays, *The New Tenant*'.[27] If instead of trying, as so many commentators have done, to disprove this claim, we take it at face-value, then something quite other emerges; not a young playwright who was (perhaps unwittingly) influenced by the continental absurdists, but one who was independently, and with direct reference to his own considerable access to a British theatrical tradition, producing a new drama that could be seen to parallel the work of Beckett and of Ionesco. This seems to me a far more useful avenue of approach. Particularly, when it is recalled that, shortly after this, Pinter is said to have written on the wall of the director's office at the Royal Court, 'le théâtre de Brecht est le théâtre de Boy Scout'[28]—a quotation from Ionesco.

25. *The Times*, 21 May 1958.

26. *The Times*, 9 March 1959.

27. *The Times*, 16 November 1960.

28. Richard Findlater (ed.), *At the Royal Court: Twenty Five Years of the English Stage Company* (London: Amber Lane Press, 1981), p. 59.

The real weight of the argument would take too long to elaborate here. Suffice it to say that the success of *Rosencrantz and Guildenstern* was made possible at the time of its first production because by then versions of the absurdist model post-*Godot* were to be found not only in the avantgarde theatre but in the mainstream. In a native theatre in which serious debate had always centred around the family unit and had been located in the room, Absurdism offered the possibility of a satiric revis-iting of territory that had been moved down the social ladder in ways which had been presaged by the work of such as Osborne. The culmi-nation of this development is to be found in the work of Alan Ayck-bourn, but would certainly take in James Saunders, Giles Cooper, and many others on the way.[29] For, at this point I return to the particular stress laid by a number of the people I quoted earlier talking about *Godot* and *Look Back in Anger*. Their success was perceived of in economic terms. Put simply, they attracted audiences, they enjoyed extended runs in the subsidised theatre and, a factor that would become increasingly important as the 1960s gave way to the 1970s, they both transferred to the commercial theatre. In 1963, Arthur Adamov remarked wickedly that 'the reason why Absurdist plays take place in No Man's Land with only two characters is primarily financial'.[30]

It was not until the 1970s, with the greater availability of state subsidy for the theatre, that theatrical models based on Brechtian epic theatre began to be found on the British stage—key texts would be David Hare's *Fanshen* of 1975, David Edgar's *Destiny* and Howard Brenton's *The Wea-pons of Happiness*, both of 1976. But, as I have argued, the question of economics is only in part one of scale; it is also about audience con-stituency and demand. Thus, to stress, as I have, the seminal importance of Beckett, and in particular *Waiting for Godot*, as the real starting-point for the new wave of the 1950s is to point to the largely unprogressive nature of that new wave, as opposed to that of a post-1968 generation of writers increasingly drawn towards the idea of a theatre that embraced the possibility of change. However, let me complete a final loop. Bertolt Brecht died in the year in which I started, 1956. After his death, it was

29. Cf. Bull, *Stage Right*, pp. 37-84, in particular, for an elaboration of this argu-ment.

30. Arthur Adamov at session on 'Commitment v the Absurd' at the Inter-national Drama Festival, Edinburgh, 1963.

discovered that he had spent part of the last months of his life making annotations in the margin of a play that he probably intended to work on a counter to, but did not live long enough, to direct—that play was Samuel Beckett's *Waiting for Godot*.[31]

31. Brecht's annotations are reproduced in Werner Hecht, *Theater der Zeit* 21.14 (1966), pp. 28-30.

Kenneth Tynan: A Mere Critic

Danny Castle

The British Library conference of December 1997 amply demonstrated Tynan's continuing importance as a critical writer of the highest order. This was not, unfortunately, as a result of my own paper but due to the length of the shadow he still casts over the study of the British Theatre. The mention of his name was frequent throughout the day as speakers repeatedly called upon his words to illustrate a point or to provide some humorous libel.

As the day progressed I realized that, as the last speaker, I was at something of a disadvantage. Paper after paper mentioned Tynan, quoted Tynan and made use of Tynan's work. In short, my colleagues used up all the best jokes. I rose from my chair, script covered in red ink, doomed to rely upon my own wit. A disastrous situation for any scholar to find himself in.

Tynan's reputation as a critic is not in doubt among theatrical historians but he is often perceived very differently by others. The headlines that reported Tynan's death in 1980 usually mentioned just two aspects of his career, inevitably aspects for which he was most notorious: namely, his status as the first person to say a particular four-letter word on television and his experimental sex-show, the 'all-nude revue', *Oh! Calcutta!*

In fact, so closely has he been associated with stage nudity that *The Concise Oxford Companion to the Theatre* goes as far as to tentatively credit him with its inauguration.[1] Another, anecdotal, illustration of his notoriety is the fact that when I told friends and family that Tynan was to be the subject of my thesis, they invariably said, with the glow of confident and complete knowledge: 'Ah, the chap that said "fuck" on

---

1. Phyllis Hartnoll (ed.), *The Concise Oxford Companion to the Theatre* (Oxford: Oxford University Press, 1972), p. 565.

telly?' (I should point out that my grandmother did not use *precisely* those words.)

Tynan courted publicity and notoriety throughout his life. While still at school he arranged a theatre conference, with *Sunday Times* critic James Agate as guest speaker, to coincide with his own performance of *Hamlet*. He went on to make a bigger splash at Oxford, where he brightened up the drab postwar years as a flamboyant, Wildean figure swanning around in purple suits and gold shirts. He also built a considerable reputation as director and actor as well as critic. His production of *Winterset* made a successful trip to Paris and his First Quarto *Hamlet* was well received and described as 'a solid achievement' by no less an authority than Donald Wolfit.[2]

After graduation, he began his professional career not as a critic but as a director. In 1949, he became Artistic Director of the Lichfield Repertory Company, relishing the challenge of putting on 24 plays in as many weeks. He ended this engagement on bad terms, finding it difficult to direct more experienced actors. Throughout 1950 and 1951 he continued to work as a director in small London theatres like the Watergate and the Arts but not with any great success.

His literary career took off with the publication in 1950 of *He That Plays the King*, a collection of reviews written while at school and university. The book was distinguished by an Orson Welles preface which was procured by an imploring Tynan appearing out of the mist one night, manuscript in hand, persuading the astonished Welles that without his participation the book would never be published. This need to be associated with a star name was typical of Tynan.

He became a full-time critic in 1951 and for the next 12 years, with the exception of one notorious acting engagement (as the Player King in Alec Guinness's disastrous 1951 *Hamlet*), Tynan earned his living almost exclusively by writing.

He wrote for the *Spectator*, the *Evening Standard* and then for a now-defunct tabloid called the *Daily Sketch*. In 1954, he replaced Ivor Brown on the *Observer* where, excepting a two-year period writing for the *New Yorker*, he stayed until 1963 when he gave up regular reviewing altogether to join the new National Theatre as Laurence Olivier's dramaturg, or Literary Manager.

He is now best remembered for his work on the *Observer*, where he quickly became essential reading and gained a reputation, which has sur-

2.   Kathleen Tynan, *The Life of Kenneth Tynan* (London: Methuen, 1987), p. 73.

vived to the present day, as the foremost descriptive writer of the age, often compared to immortals like Hazlitt and Shaw. People often remember the 1950s in terms of Tynan's reviews, sometimes not able to say with complete certainty whether they recall a production itself or whether it is Tynan's decription of it that has implanted itself in the mind. He has handed to posterity an invaluable record of the theatre of the 1950s.

It was for the *Observer* that Tynan wrote his famous scathing attacks on the contemporary theatrical scene with what he saw as its preponderance of middle-class comedies and preoccupation with French windows. Well-known examples of these articles are 'Apathy'[3] in which he savaged 'the peculiar nullity of our drama's prevalent genre, the Loamshire play' and 'Dead Language' in which he bemoaned the lack of a new English masterpiece for 300 years:

> When the London theatre takes to its bed, the habit of criticism is to scourge the invalid; the sickroom resounds with bullying cries of 'Who are the new English playwrights?' A more acute inquiry might be 'Who were the old ones?'[4]

He sometimes devoted an entire column to one of his pet causes. For example, 'Payment Deferred' attacked the failure of the government to establish a national theatre seven years after the approval of the National Theatre Bill in 1949. He concluded the piece with an echo of Matthew Arnold: 'The Act is Irresistible; implement the Act!'[5]

Tynan was not always such a campaigning legislator, tirelessly lambasting the theatrical establishment (or, depending on your viewpoint, banging on about Brecht week after week). The early reviews in *He That Plays the King* and the *Spectator* were overwhelmingly of the classics and concerned themselves with actors' performances and very little else.

The *Evening Standard* pieces began to include increasingly more reviews of new plays and from then on he concerned himself more and more with literary and theatrical movements; general essays on the state of the theatre appeared more frequently. This trend continued during his tenure at the *Observer*.

However, when he came to make a selection of reviews to be included in *Curtains*, a compilation of his work of the 1950s, the emphasis for the years up to 1956 was on classics and revivals and disregarded the

3. *Observer*, 31 October 1954.
4. *Observer*, 21 November 1954.
5. *Observer*, 1 January 1956.

wealth of new work that he had reviewed in his columns. Furthermore, paragraphs to do with direction and historical context were often edited or excised, thus emphasising the performance aspect still further.[6]

However, the second half of the decade is represented in the book by many more reviews of new plays. The book reproduces five pieces on new plays which opened before that date together with five polemical essays from the *Observer*, the period after that date is represented by 14 reviews of new plays and just one instructive essay.

Tynan was plainly of the opinion that the new work being produced in the London theatre in the second half of the decade (that is, the period after *Waiting for Godot* and *Look Back in Anger*) was of a superior standard to that of the previous five years. *Curtains* (reissued by Penguin as *Tynan on Theatre* in 1964) is still a widely-read book and one to which many people turn to gain a flavour of 1950s theatre. Such an influential critic disregarding the new drama of the first half of the decade in this manner has surely contributed to the perception of that period as a 'cultural desert'.

Tynan was notorious in the 1950s for his proselytising support for the work of Bertolt Brecht. Tynan wrote often on Brecht, especially after 1956 when the Berliner Ensemble visited Britain, but he also wrote in-sistently on other campaigns such as the abolition of the censorship and the foundation of a national theatre.

Brecht is often credited with (or blamed for) turning Tynan on to Marxism and Tynan was mocked as something of a 'champagne socialist' by his contemporaries. Whether or not Marxist philosophy penetrated his private life, it is true that after first seeing the Berliner Ensemble in 1955 he found himself, in his writing, increasingly concerned with a play's effect on society and economics.

However, the germs of this attitude were present earlier. The frustra-tion he had been feeling with the French window brigade was precisely because of their plays' narrow social range and the chasm between them and the society that he felt they ought to reflect. He still recognised that there was room for both kinds of drama: 'We need plays about cabmen *and* demi-gods, plays about politicians, warriors *and* grocers'.[7]

By January 1956, having seen the Berliner Ensemble, he was to make

6.   See James Lee De Young, 'A Study of the Theatrical Criticism of Kenneth Tynan 1951-63' (unpublished doctoral dissertation, University of Minnesota, 1974), pp. 53, 88.
7.   *Observer*, 31 October 1954.

a further step towards Marxism in his thinking and express explicitly that the best drama is that which concerns the whole of society. He wrote: 'Cornered individuals are always good meat for drama; but cornered communities can be even better. Let the author put his hero into a social context and we are held at once'.[8]

However, Tynan had been aware of Brecht and his work for several years and one might suspect that the real impact of seeing the Ensemble was more to do with the striking production than the Marxist philosophy. Another reason that the company impressed him so greatly was that, in the Berliner Ensemble, he saw a model for a British national theatre.

Tynan repeatedly campaigned in the *Observer* for such an institution, emphasising the importance of public subsidy;[9] drawing envious attention to the different situations in France, Sweden and Germany,[10] as well as outlining his ideas for what the role of such a theatre in Britain would be.[11]

It is often suggested that Tynan abandoned his vocation when he gave up regular criticism in order to work for the National. There seems to be an impression that he wasted time there that would have been best spent in writing. Most of his obituarists and many of those interviewed for the 1982 *Reputations* TV programme on Tynan's life were of this opinion.

Through his theatrical criticism of the 1950s, he had set out his manifesto, so to speak. He had relentlessly picked apart the offerings of the day but pointed out why, in his view, they failed. He was, by Shaw's definition, a *great* critic because he not only reviewed what was in front of him but also saw what was *not* happening in the theatre.

However, it is obvious from his writing that Tynan was a man longing to be *doing* things. On the subject of the lack of a national theatre, for example, he was explicit that the money recommended in the 1949 Bill should be released, that the Old Vic should be the temporary home of the National Theatre until a new building could be completed and also that Laurence Olivier should be appointed Director.[12] This was active campaigning (which eventually bore fruit).

8.   *Observer*, 29 January 1956.
9.   *Observer*, 26 October 1958.
10. *Observer*, 2 January 1955; 30 January 1955; 9 March 1958.
11. *Observer*, 22 December 1957; 27 December 1959.
12. *Observer*, 1 January 1956, 11 March 1962.

He did not, in the *Observer*, go so far as to publicly proclaim 'and I should be made dramaturg' but he suggested that appointment in a private letter to Olivier. Tynan's letter has, unfortunately, been lost but Olivier replied to it positively on 21 August 1962, concluding: 'God, *anything* to get you off that *Observer*!'

In the 1950s he had held a position comparable to that of dramaturg at Ealing film studios. In 1956–58, he acted as Script Editor, commissioning scripts and dealing with writers. But he had little influence there—the scripts he commissioned were never filmed and his suggestions for directors were not listened to. He always felt he had failed and in December 1958 a long, ironic letter to Michael Balcon, the Director of Ealing Studios, expressed the frustration he had felt in the job.

> at my suggestion [...] you spent large sums of money on writers whose work you never used and books you never turned into films [...] If Ealing should collapse, let not my name be absent from the list of those who brought it to its knees.[13]

This episode may have affected his later work at the National by making him so determined to have an effect there. Many of his colleagues spoke of his politicking ways and his devious, though often transparent, resolution in pursuing certain projects.[14]

In the Balcon letter, Tynan criticized the studio's policy of using only its own directors which resulted in projects being turned down: for example, *Look Back in Anger* which had the director Tony Richardson as part of the package.

Tynan's frustration at his impotence in the face of policies and practices carved in stone is almost tangible. Given this, it is hardly surprising that when he was offered the chance to help form the National Theatre Company from its inception, in a position of greater influence at the right hand of its Director, he leaped at the chance.

Furthermore, as I pointed out earlier, he began his career as a theatrical practitioner and was for many years a frustrated producer. As we have seen, his writings on the British theatre were often prescriptive and the post at the National Theatre was an ideal way for him to put into practice the views expounded in his weekly columns.

13. Kathleen Tynan (ed.), *Kenneth Tynan: Letters* (London: Weidenfeld & Nicholson, 1994), pp. 220-28.

14. John Dexter, interview with Kathleen Tynan, 1982 (transcript in Tynan Archive).

Far from *abandoning* his vocation, it was when he became a dramaturg that he *found* it. Many of those who worked with him at the National describe him as a natural impresario who directed at one remove and who had a particular flair for 'packaging', putting together directors, actors and designers who complemented each other in fresh, exciting ways.[15]

Tynan was the first dramaturg in England. His basic function was to advise on repertoire, and to find plays for the Director to consider by reading new scripts and rediscovering old and neglected plays. He was also to act as in-house critic for productions in rehearsal.

Some directors, like Michael Blakemore, found his observations and notes very useful but others resented the interference of one until recently regarded as 'the enemy'. The theatrical culture in Britain was very different from that in Germany where the dramaturg was an important and recognized member of the production staff. 'Literary Managers' are now much more common in this country but rarely do they have the wide-ranging brief that Tynan enjoyed at the National.

While at the National he retained his commitment to political or socially relevant works although he had limited success in his campaigns for such plays. For example, for the whole of his 10 years at the National he tried, to no avail, to put on a play about the General Strike and he famously failed to convince the Board that Hochhuth's *Soldiers* was a suitable play for production at Britain's National Theatre.[16] However, it is mainly due to Tynan that important snapshots of society like Trevor Griffiths's *The Party* and Peter Nichols's *The National Health* were produced.

His enthusiasm for Brecht also remained unabated and immediately upon his appointment he began to arrange a visit by the Berliner Ensemble, now led by Brecht's widow, Helene Weigel. The visit finally took three years to achieve. He also spent an inordinate amount of time and energy in correspondence regarding the National's own production of *Mother Courage*, not only with the Lord Chamberlain's Office but also with the Brecht estate, which zealously guarded the author's reputation.

15. For example, Derek Granger and Adrian Mitchell, interviews with the author.

16. Tynan eventually managed to produce *Soldiers* independently at the New Theatre in 1968.

The long and tortuous correspondence is contained in the Tynan Archive.[17]

Tynan might be criticized for using his position to put on works by his favourite writer. But he did also spend a great a deal of time and energy on productions for which he displayed no particular keenness in the quest to present the 'spectrum of world drama' that he had always said the National Theatre should be in a position to perform.

Tynan had been an outspoken critic of the Theatre of Cruelty and of much avant-garde physical theatre:

> It was Brook's *US* which really sabotaged any chance of proper political theatre in this country. It wasn't about the millions of people who were actually being killed. It was about the agonies of Hampstead intellectuals about the war. Indulgent and ridiculous... An immense act of hubris.[18]

Fernando Arrabal's work fell into this category, although in a more absurdist vein, but in spite of his personal misgivings Tynan felt obliged to promote the work of, in his opinion, an important European drama-tist in order to fulfil the National's repertory brief. His intense dislike of Arrabal's *Labyrinth* did not diminish his enthusiasm for the inclusion of the author's work in the repertoire.[19] Tynan spent five years trying to get his *The Architect and the Emperor of Assyria* put on at the Old Vic, digging it out whenever a gap in the schedules appeared. Finally, in 1970, he succeeded in this endeavour but unfortunately, the play was a disastrous flop.

Despite his growing need for a play to have a social and economic context, he never lost his fascination for actors and performances. He was always interested in all kinds of performances, including such things as bullfights and cricket matches. He was especially fascinated by *lone* performers like matadors and batsmen as well as orators and actors.

One of the contradictions of Tynan's character was his adulation of stars together with his commitment to the ensemble principle on which the National Theatre Company was founded. Many memoranda survive on the subject of the Company in which he made detailed recommen-dations for the company and planned future strategies. However, such was his reputation that there is a story that John Dexter once made a

---

17. The *Mother Courage* saga is a subject for a separate article: space does not permit me to go into detail here.

18. Tynan, interview with Nicholas Tomalin (transcript in Tynan Archive).

19. *Observer*, 23 June 1968.

barbed joke to a struggling actor: 'You'll have to do better than that, dear, or Ken Tynan will have Richard Burton in here'.

This star-policy/ensemble dichotomy was the cause of a dispute between Tynan and William Gaskill, who also saw the Berliner Ensemble as the model to follow. Tynan often wanted to bring in guest actors and directors (for example, it was Tynan who had the idea of hiring Franco Zeffirelli to direct *Much Ado About Nothing*) but Gaskill demurred. On the casting of his production of *Mother Courage*, Gaskill wrote in his autobiography: 'Tynan had fancy ideas about Anna Magnani but I was opposed to his star policy'.[20]

Later, Gaskill was 'appalled' to find that in the *Mother Courage* programme Tynan had printed two large photos of the Berliner Ensemble's Helene Weigel in that famous role.[21] He was angry not only because it created an impossible task for the National's Madge Ryan who could not be expected to live up to the Weigel legend, but also because Tynan's action went against Gaskill's whole way of working. Having huge photos of one actor relegated the rest of the ensemble to supporting players; Gaskill aspired to a situation where the company itself would be the star that audiences wanted to see.

Because of this obvious contradiction in Tynan's theatrical thought it is not surprising that, as well as political docudramas, Tynan pushed for big star performances from the biggest theatrical star of all, who happened to be his employer. Tynan's biggest successes in politicking and persuasion at the National were also among Laurence Olivier's greatest triumphs on the stage: for example, *Othello* and *Long Day's Journey Into Night*.

Tynan's biggest regret in his life, according to his biographer and widow Kathleen Tynan, was that he never directed a theatrical production in his mature working life. His last production was in 1951 at the age of 24. The final years at the National represented a succession of frustrated theatrical ambitions for Tynan.

The possibility was raised, circa 1972, of codirecting with Olivier a production of *King Lear*. Tynan made pages of notes which survive in the Archive but the project came to nothing. Later, when asked if he knew of Tynan's desire to direct, Olivier paused for a long time before replying, strangely, 'Why didn't I want him to?' and going on to say that

20. William Gaskill, *A Sense of Direction* (London: Faber and Faber, 1988), p. 59.
21. Memo to Tynan, 14 May 1965.

he had probably been jealous and did not want Tynan to have 'all that kudos'.[22]

Soon after Hall joined the National as Olivier's co-Director in 1973, Tynan asked him if he could direct Ronald Firbank's *The Princess Zoubaroff*. Hall had felt the previous year that 'there is only one person whom I categorically… could not work with—Ken Tynan'.[23] Despite this, he suggested that Tynan coordinate a themed season to run in the Lyttelton Theatre when the South Bank building opened (then scheduled for 1974). This idea caught Tynan's enthusiasm and the two men corresponded in detail on the possible content of such a season.

Tynan's directorial ambitions were frustrated once again, this time by the delays in the building of the National's South Bank home. The project had been shelved long before the Lyttelton was finally completed in 1976 by which time Tynan's failing health had obliged him to move to the warmer climate of California.

He ended his career and his life in Los Angeles, once again writing for a living—mainly his celebrated series of theatrical and showbiz profiles for the *New Yorker*. The series included pieces on Ralph Richardson and Louise Brooks and several were later collected and published as *Show People*.[24]

He began his career as a director of some promise but early disappointments in that sphere combined with phenomenal and immediate success as a critic decided the course of his career in the 1950s.

While still a critic, he flirted with a career in the film industry at Ealing Studios in 1956–58 and also enjoyed a brief spell as a TV producer for ATV, responsible for the arts series *Tempo* in 1961. It was not until the creation of the National Theatre in 1963 that he found a role of sufficient practical influence to justify giving up regular reviewing, a profession by which he had not only made his living but which also had given him a powerful voice in the theatrical world.

His work at the National was his opportunity to put into practice what he had preached in his columns. It was also where he might fulfil the directorial ambitions he had nursed for many years. While at the National, he acted as an impresario in bringing his pet projects *Soldiers* and

22. Olivier, interview with Kathleen Tynan, 1983. (Tape and transcript in Tynan Archive.)

23. Peter Hall, *Peter Hall's Diaries* (ed. John Goodwin; London: Hamish Hamilton, 1983), p. 3.

24. London: Weidenfeld & Nicolson, 1980.

Oh! Calcutta! to the stage. He did the same with *Carte Blanche* in 1976 but he never directed again after 1951.

Tynan's place in theatrical history is assured thanks to his critical writings which were not so much theatre criticism as ammunition in his campaign to enrich the British Theatre. The other aspects of his career are also fascinating and his story of frustrated desire and ambition is an instructive one which adds poignancy and weight to his later work.

Finally, Tynan's contribution to the first 10 years of the National Theatre was a crucial one. He instigated the still fledgling tradition of dramaturgy that exists in Britain today and brought to public attention the work of otherwise obscure authors, adding an eclectic and modern attitude to the repertoire.

The 1950s: Birthplace of the National Theatres of Great Britain

Fiona Kavanagh Fearon

In 1949, one hundred and six years after Effingham Wilson first suggested a National Theatre for Great Britain, the dream finally seemed to be a possible reality when the National Theatre Act agreed to put aside £1,000,000 for the building of a National Theatre. The principle of governement funding for a National Theatre had initially been agreed upon in 1913, but the First World War had intervened. Although a site was purchased in Bloomsbury in the inter-war years no funding could be made available, and it was not until 1949 that a government finally agreed upon a budget to build a National Theatre. It took another 14 years, until 1963, before the National Theatre Company became a reality, and another 27 years, 1976, before a building for the Company was actually complete.

The question has to be asked, why did it take so long to create a National Theatre in Great Britain? Why in 1848, when Effingham Wilson first suggested the idea, did England not have a National Theatre, when it had the British Museum, the British Library and the National Gallery? Why did it take another hundred years before a British Government would agree to fund a National Theatre, when the French Government had given a subsidy to the Comedie Francaise since 1802 and the Irish Free State Government subsidized the Abbey from 1925? Even when that one million pounds had been agreed upon by the British Government in 1949, it still did not materialize for more than 10 years, and its removal was threatened more than once.

Obviously it would be simplistic to suggest there were only one or two reasons for this long delay. What I would like to discuss is how the developments in British theatre in the 1950s particularly prohibited and encouraged the development of the National Theatre. One of the key reasons for the delay in the development of the National in the late 1950s, was the existence of two theatres which already satisfied in some way ideas about what a National Theatre should be. The Royal Court in London satisfied the support of new British writing, and the Stratford Memorial Theatre, which became the Royal Shakespeare Company in 1961, satisfied the support of the work of Shakespeare. These were two of the main prerequisites of the plan for a National Theatre first formulated by Harley Granville Barker and William Archer in 1907. Governments in the 1950s must have reasoned the need for an institution like the National, when a major part of its brief was already being satisfied by two other theatres.

Britain was the birthplace of possibly the greatest playwright the world has ever know, and even in 1949 there was no theatre where Shakespeare's work was permanently on display. In 1848 Effingham Wilson was looking for a theatre to celebrate Shakespeare's achievement, and by 1916, the anniversary of his death, a movement to literally enshrine his work in a monument had only narrowly been avoided. Instead Archer and Granville Barker had formulated a scheme that involved not only the performance of all of Shakespeare's work, but the best of world theatre and the advocacy of new playwriting. Gradually as the century progressed two other British theatres became closely associated with the promotion of Shakespeare and the advocacy of new writing, and in the 1950s both were reaching a zenith.

When Kenneth Tynan asked Sir Laurence Olivier for the job of being dramaturg to the National Theatre company in 1962, he must have only superficially been aware that his role as coordinator of the repertoire had already been mapped out by the events of the previous decade. Olivier's response to Tynan's request was initially disbelief at the cheek of the famously vituperative critic, and Olivier's letter from the Chichester Festival Theatre accepting Tynan's offer, has a hand written coda under the typed letter, Olivier saying, '*God—any*thing to get you off that *Observer!*'[1]. However Tynan had been an ardent supporter of the National Theatre, through the barren years of the 1950s, and his enthusiasm and knowledge were probably just as significant encouragements for Olivier to make his appointment, as the desire to remove his venomous criticism from the public domain.

1.   Letter from Laurence Olivier to Kenneth Tynan, from Chichester Festival Theatre, dated 21 August 1962. Kenneth Tynan Letters, National Theatre File 1, British Library.

Repertoire management of companies as large as the National Theatre and the Royal Shakespeare Company seems to be a constant struggle to balance the search for interesting new plays or translations against casting from within the company and finding roles for star performers who are interested in playing with one of the National companies for a short time. Colin Chambers, ex-literary Manager of the RSC and Purni Morel, Assistant Literary Manager of the Royal National Theatre, have both talked about the somewhat tortuous process by which a play gets to the stage of either of these two theatres.[2] A play might be suggested to them by either a director, actor, agent or playwright, read and assessed by readers employed within the company, then a suggested director or lead actor might be asked to read it. If it is a foreign play, another translation or series of translations might be sought. It then might be suggested for the repertoire up to two years in advance, and then be thrown out for a number of different reasons—such as the company might already be doing a play by that playwright or one of his contemporaries, it might prove impossible to spare a star performer for two such demanding parts, the right lead may not become available, or a director that is interested might not be found, or things as mundane as the suggested director gets a job in television or the lead actress gets pregnant. Kenneth Tynan's job between 1963 and 1973, from the numerous memos and planned schedules in his archive, seems to have been just as complicated, and it is often difficult to see any conscious planning when one is at the mercy of such vagaries.

However Kenneth Tynan's wife, Kathleen, did feel he had a 'blueprint' for the repertoire of the new Naitonal theatre. She suggested that it was 'to put on the best of world drama, a spectrum which could cover, as the Archer/Granville-Barker scheme had proposed, new and modern plays, revivals of English classics, including Shakespeare, and new, modern and classic foreign plays.'[3] The only major difference between this outline and the Archer/Granville-Barker *Proposed Shakespeare Memorial National Theatre* handbook, is the distinct absence of Shakespeare as the dominant author of the theatre.[4] Kathleen uses the phrase 'the best of

2.   Colin Chambers, Keynote address, 'True to Form' Conference, University of Hull, 12, 13, 14 September, 1997, and conversation with Purni Morel at the same conference.

3.   Kathleen Tynan, *The Life of Kenneth Tynan* (London: Methuen, 1988), p. 219.

4.   See Geoffrey Whitworth, *The Making of A National Theatre* (London: Faber &

world drama', and it is clear from the plays that were actually performed at the National between 1963 and 1973 that Tynan emphasized the National's role as the only theatre whose express purpose was to promote plays from around the world, most of which were performed in translation. He also felt the National had a responsibility to encourage the best international directors, actors and companies to perform for a British audience. This is very different to the concept of some other National Theatres, particularly Ireland and France, which are seen primarily as theatres for the promotion and encouragement of plays and performers that are particularly indicative of the home culture. The original concept of the National in Britain had been almost entirely as a response to the lack of a formal institution to promote Shakespeare, but by 1963 the National could not claim that role for itself. The RSC was already doing that job very effectively.

Although 'new and modern plays' are included in Tynan's 'blue print', in reality finding new British playwrights was not always that easy. Although Tynan tried to attract new playwrights and promote new plays, his major Briitish successes were rare, though they did include Stoppard's *Rosencrantz and Guildernstern are Dead* and *The National Health* by Peter Nichols. Tynan felt the best new British writing was elsewhere. Arden, Wesker, Edward Bond, and David Storey were at the Royal Court, and Pinter was at the RSC. Therefore the National's programme had to revert to the wider spectrum of world theatre or adopt a deliberate in house style, like Brecht or Stanislavski. In fact a consistent directorial style would have been impossible, as Elsom points out, 'Between October 1963 and October 1974, no less than 41 directors were given productions at the National Theatre (NT), 25 of them directing only one play.'[5] When Olivier appointed William Gaskill and John Dexter as Associate Directors he cannot have anticipated that their stay with him and the National would have been so short, Gaskill leaving in 1965 and Dexter in 1967. Peter Lewis points out that 'House Style', 'was never mentioned at the Old Vic', and he suggests that both Gaskill and Dexter were frustrated by attempts of the National to create an ensemble which were then ruined by the introduction of guest stars and guest directors.[6]

Faber, 1951), p. 83, from *The Proposed Shakespeare Memorial National Theatre: An Illustrated Handbook, 1909*, produced by the Shakespeare National Theatre Committee.

5.　John Elsom, *Post-War British Theatre* (London: Routledge & Kegan Paul, 1976), p. 165.

6.　Peter Lewis, *A Dream Made Concrete* (London: Methuen, 1990), p. 32.

Tynan may have felt that by introducing new directors, especially visitors from the Berliner Ensemble or Zeffirelli he was expanding the European connection, that was the National's strongest claim to funding. Since the RSC satisfied the function of being the playhouse of the national playwright, and the Royal Court seemed to have a monopoly on some of the best new British writing, the National had to fulfil the other functions laid down in the Archer/Granville Barker handbook, of producing the best of European and world drama, old and new. A strong argument can be made for the fact that developments in the Royal Shakespeare Company and the Royal Court significantly effected the type of theatre Tynan felt he should promote in developing the repertoire. It is not simply that his inclination was toward European plays, but the strength of the National's argument for its existance and funding were in covering areas of the repertoire not already covered by existing companies.

When Peter Hall was first invited to direct at the Stratford Memorial Theatre in 1956 it was already becoming clear that in order to maintain the quality of the annual Shakespeare Festivals, that Stratford had been holding since 1879, it would need to extend its season and find a London home. Antony Quayle had been arguing for a London base for some time because he felt that once the National Theatre arrived Stratford would lose its premiere position:

> The National Theatre would be well subsidized: actors could live at home in London: they were not confined to a diet of Shakespeare; they could range through the centuries; they could pick their plays from any foreign country they wanted, while we were stuck in Warwickshire like rabbits.[7]

In 1958 when Hall and Fordham Flower planned their own version of a national theatre, no more than a corner stone had been laid for the real National Theatre, and that had moved three times since 1951. Although Hall and Flower did not seem to acknowledge the potential detrimental effects of their plans on the National, Hall did acknowledge that the imminent threat of the National becoming a reality, and its possible detrimental effects on Stratford were among his major concerns when forming the RSC.[8] However, his express purpose of transforming Stratford

7.   Anthony Quayle, *A Time to Speak* (London: Barrie and Jenkins, 1990), quoted by Stephen Fay, *Power Play: The Life and Times of Peter Hall* (London: Hodder and Stoughton, 1995), p. 112.

8.   See Peter Hall, *Making an Exhibition of Myself* (London: Sinclair Stevenson, 1993), p. 147.

into 'one of the world's major permanent companies, on a size and a scale previously not seen in Britain' seems much more ambitious than a simple desire to survive the still not established presence of the National Theatre.[9]

By 1959 when Olivier came to Stratford to play Coriolanus, Hall was not only heir apparent at Stratford, his ambitious plans for the redevelopment of the Shakespeare Memorial Theatre as an all year round theatre with a London base were well under way. Olivier had unofficially been appointed as Artisitic Director of the National Theatre in 1958 and the two men must have been aware that the ambitious plans for Stratford would put the two companies in direct competition. In 1959 the representatives of the two companies started sensitive negotiations for amalagmation.[10] During rehearsals for Coriolanus Olivier asked Hall to work with him on the as yet unformed National. Lewis says that Hall rebuffed Olivier's offer of partnership with the words, 'Sorry, Larry, I'm immensely flattered but I'm going to make it on my own as Number One'.[11] Despite this refusal, amalgamation was discussed seriously for the next three years, and at one point Hall even invited Olivier to work under him as the leader of the combined companies.[12] Olivier and Hall seem to be two diametrically opposed characters, Olivier constantly deprecating his own intelligence, even in personal letters he described himself as a 'non-intellectual',[13] while Hall's reputation as an intellectual giant, who enjoyed 'power and being ruthless in his manipulation of it' at Stratford, seems incompatible with the last great actor manager. However in his autobiography, Hall felt that 'in spite of rebuffs and misunderstandings, relations with Olivier continued to be personally cordial'.[14] Olivier does not specifically mention the *Coriolanus* confrontation in his autobiography, though on learning of Hall's appointment to the National he says that, 'It was a good thing now that our

9. John Elsom and Nicholas Tomalin, *The History of the National Theatre* (London: Jonathan Cape, 1978), pp. 119-20.

10. See *Making an Exhibition of Myself*, pp. 200-201.

11. Lewis, *A Dream Made Concrete*, p. 6, see also Hall, *Making an Exhibition of Myself*, p. 170.

12. See Elsom and Tomalin, *The History of the National Theatre*, p. 122.

13. Letter from Laurence Olivier to Kenneth Tynan, 'Sat Night 12 Dec', 1970, Tynan Letters, National Theatre File 1, British Library.

14. *Making an Exhibition of Myself*, p. 171.

rivalry had claimed so stoutly to be a friendly one'.[15] The use of the word 'claimed', perhaps indicates more clearly the kind of relationship the two had in private. Personal letters from Olivier to Hall, during the tortuous negotiations between the two companies in 1962 show some of the personal tension and venom behind the superficially friendly relationship. Stephen Fay says:

> Behind their masks, Hall's relationship with Olivier was less good-natured than it appeared. Both claimed that they were on the same side; both felt they ought to be allies; but instinctively they were competitors. Olivier's discussions with Hall during rehearsals for Coriolanus in 1959, when Hall refused to join him at the National Theatre, coloured their subsequent relationship.[16]

Relations deteriorated between the two men when the Chancellor of the Exchequer, Selwyn Lloyd, announced in March 1961 that £400,000 would be allotted for funding the Old Vic, regional theatres and Stratford, at the expense of a still non-existent National Theatre. The threat of loosing a National Theatre, when they had seemed so close, threw the pro-National Theatre lobby into operation and in the latter half of 1961 the London County Council agreed to match the million pounds promised by the Government in the 1949 Act.[17] Selwyn Lloyd immediately switched allegiance and £400,000 was promised to combine the National with Sadler's Wells on the South Bank. As Peter Lewis puts it, the RSC were already 'acting as if it were de facto a national theatre company', and one can understand the Government's reservation about funding a non existent, unproven company when the RSC was fulfilling many of the functions of a national theatre laid down in Granville Barker and Archer's 1907 handbook. Irving Wardle compared the two companies in 1966, saying:

> ...in fact they are wildly different organizations both in policy and in official status. The seeds of their difference are contained in their separate origins—one beginning as an expressive need in search of an institution, the other beginning as an institution in search of an expressive need.[18]

15. Laurence Olivier, *Confessions of an Actor* (London: Weidenfeld and Nicolson, 1982), p. 247.

16. Fay, *Power Play*, p. 170

17. Lewis, *A Dream Made Concrete*, pp. 12-13

18. Irving Wardle, 'London's Subsidized Companies', *Tulane Drama Review*, 2.2 (T34), (1966), pp. 105-19 (107).

Around January or February of 1962 Olivier wrote a 12 page diatribe to Hall in reaction to the machinations of Hall and associates in trying to remove funding altogether from the National Theatre. Olivier was livid;

> The trouble as I see it (and have from the beginnings of your schemes) is that you have really set out to be the Nat Th (sic) yourself, or if you prefer it, for Stratford to develop a position for itself as heir to the throne, or else to make such a throne unnecessary.[19]

Superficially the relationship between Hall and Olivier must have improved after this 1962 low. In September 1963 Peter Hall wrote to Kenneth Tynan to make his apologies for not being able to attend a conference Tynan was organising. He concluded by saying, 'And very best wishes for the National Theatre Opening. These wishes are genuine & full of self-interest—I believe that if you thrive, we all have a chance of thriving'.[20]

The financial future of the National had been rescued, but Olivier and Hall were in competition for funding and actors now, and Kenneth Tynan seems to be constantly aware that the RSC had already established a style and a repertoire that the National had to compete with in the audiences mind.

The RSC may have lost out financially but artistically they outshone the National in the first few years, the association with Pinter in *The Collection* (1962) and *The Homecoming* (1965), *The Wars of the Roses* in 1963, followed by the complete cycle of the History plays in 1964, David Warner's contemporary *Hamlet* (1965), as well as the Theatre of Cruelty season and *Marat Sade* at the Aldwych (1964). The RSC had a house dramatist, a strongly lead directors theatre with a desire to academically reassess Shakespeare, and a proven ability to experiment with new forms and styles of theatre, and a living, breathing, working ensemble. No wonder Tynan had a tendency to sound rather sensitive when discussing the National's competitive relationship with the RSC.[21] The RSC had appropriated Shakespeare as its major playwright, thus denying the National Theatre this element of the original design envisaged by

19. Fay, *Power Play*, p. 180

20. Letter to 'My dear Ken' signed Peter, from Avoncliffe, Stratford Upon Avon. Signature of Peter Hall checked against other copies in the Tynan Letters. National Theatre, File 1, Tynan Letters, British Library.

21. Memo from Tynan to Laurence Olivier, 3 January 1967, Tynan Letters, British Library, see also *Kenneth Tynan Letters* (ed. Kathleen Tynan; London: Minerva, 1995), p. 376.

Archer and Granville Barker. Therefore the National's programme had to revert to the other elements of the plan, the wider spectrum of world theatre and new plays.

Of the 98 new productions performed on the stage of the National Theatre between 1963 and 1973, 47 of them have their origin abroad, either from their playwright or their director. Of those only two were American, which means that the overwhelming majority of those plays were written in languages other than English and translated for performance on the English stage. Plays like *Much Ado About Nothing* or *Coriolanus* when they are directed by continental European directors, such as Franco Zeffirelli or the Berliner Ensemble directors, Manfred Wekwerth and Joachim Tenschert, should also be seen to come from abroad, as well as the more obvious visiting production of Zeffirelli's 1964 *Amleto* or the Berliner Ensemble tour of 1965.

Among Tynan's letters is a list of National Theatre productions that Tynan appears to have marked according to who originated the productions. At the top of the page, handwritten, is 'Prod we'wd not have done without me'(sic).[22] In the latter part of 1970, when the National was experiencing a critical low, Tynan sought to place the blame anywhere except at his own door. This list of productions was probably part of a series trying to justify Tynan's importance to the Company, at a time when relations between Olivier and Tynan were low. This is an example of one of their memos, Olivier to Tynan in April 1970 after a row:

> If you want to consult with me you know perfectly well that you may do so at any time and welcome, but what is getting less and less welcome are these snappy notes of yours. I don't like snappy notes going about this organisation—it is much better to go and see somebody and talk reasonably, in fact, have a 'consultation'.[23]

Memos continue to appear in a similar vein between 1970 and 1973, when both men had agreed to leave the National. Tynan's letters and memos suggest that he was the major instigator behind the visit of the Berliner Ensemble in 1965, the force behind the choice of Zeffirelli for director of *Much Ado About Nothing* in 1965, and as reader of plays and dramaturg he felt it his responsibility to constantly extend the breadth of

---

22. Undated,Tynan Letters, National Theatre File 1, British Library.
23. Memo From:LO To:KT, Copy to D.G., 24/4/1970, Tynan Letters, National Theatre File 1, British Library.

the repertory, suggesting new British playwrights like Arden or Osborne as well as European playwrights such as Schnitzler, Jarry, or the young Vaclav Havel.[24] The annotated list among his letters attributes plays like *Andorra, A Flea in her Ear, The Dance of Death, Danton's Death* and *Saturday, Sunday, Monday,* to Kenneth Tynan. Tynan's provisional figures at the end of the page attribute 40 out of the 80 productions to his instigation. At least four other people are given credit for the choice of plays, but even with Kathleen's conservative estimation of 32 plays instigated by Tynan, he is clearly deserving of the title 'architect of the repertory'.[25]

I would argue that Tynan's choices as dramaturg and repertory manager were limited in many ways by the National's relationship to the RSC and the emerging new British playwrights of the 1950s. By challenging the right of the National for funding and repertory choices the RSC probably mobilized the National Theatre movement out of the stagnation of the 1950s, enabling the National to find its identity through contrast and comparison. Irving Wardle was right in defining the National as an institution in search of a need, and the RSC as a need in search of an institution. The 1950s gave definition to the Shakespeare Memorial Theatre in contrast to the angry young men of Sloane Square, and inspired Peter Hall to reform the Company as a more contemporary institution for the celebration of Shakespeare in the 1960s. Tynan's experience as a critic in the 1950s, the development of his influences and taste from Brecht to Beckett, cannot help but have influenced his choices in the development of the repertory of the National in the 1960s. More importantly, developments in the English Stage Company and the RSC in the 1950s always forced Tynan to be constantly looking over his shoulder in the 1960s, seeking to justify the funding of the National Theatre as the only theatre whose mandate expressly included the provision of the best plays from around the world.

24. See *Kenneth Tynan Letters*, pp. 275, 287, 312-13.

25. The four others referred to in Tynan's notes are only referred to by a letter, F, M, S or C, which seems most likely to have been Olivier. The other letters should refer to the other associate directors, but the only obvious connection is 'F', perhaps signifying Frank Dunlop.

Apart from *Look Back in Anger,* what *else* was worrying the Lord Chamberlain's Office in 1956?*

Kathryn Johnson

Much the same, one finds, as had concerned his predecessors in the office of Lord Chamberlain for many years: he was worried about displays of female nudity, about vice-melodramas, and increasingly about plays with a homosexual theme or with homosexual characters. *Look Back in Anger* itself was licensed at the end of March without much fuss, after a fairly small number of cuts had been agreed, and despite the file on the play having been consulted twice as often as any other in the Lord Chamberlain's Plays correspondence since the papers came to the British Library, there was very little at the time that marked the play out as a watershed of twentieth-century English drama.

Only one play was absolutely refused a licence in 1956 and that was *The Life of Christ*, which I will deal with in more detail later. Three plays had been banned in 1955 and four in 1957; the figures were going down steadily from the high point of 15 or 16 plays a year refused a licence by Lord Cromer in the early 1930s. In 1956 itself there were 17 of the so-called 'Waiting Box' plays, scripts which for various reasons were said not to have met the conditions for the issuing of a licence. In most cases, this was simply because the place and date of first production had not

*   This paper is an amended and augmented version of a lecture given at the British Library/University of Sheffield seminar on 6 December 1997. The author wishes to express her particular thanks to her colleagues in the Department of Manuscripts who patiently waited for her to finish writing the revised version before moving the Lord Chamberlain's Plays Correspondence and all their associated indexes to the new building at St Pancras. Dedicated, with affection and respect to my friend and colleague, Patricia Basing, on her retirement from the Department of Manuscripts, 28 August 1998

been supplied, but in a significant minority, this omission was not a matter of carelessness but of calculation. The Theatres Act of 1843 specified that a place and date of publication *must* be specified before a licence could issue, but producers unwilling to risk the expense of booking a venue and performers on the strength of a script which the Lord Chamberlain's Office (LCO) might refuse to license occasionally tried to evade this condition by deliberately submitting the script without these details, to test the water, so to speak, without getting soaking wet. Although by the 1950s, the Lord Chamberlain and his staff quite often agreed to see authors and producers who wished to discuss a script, it should not be forgotten that he had absolute power under the act to refuse a licence to a play, and even to withdraw a licence from a play in production for any reason whatsoever, without giving a reason.[1]

The Lord Chamberlain in 1956 was the Earl of Scarbrough.[2] He was not a particularly artistic man or a liberal thinker, nor even a great theatre-goer, but he devoted a great deal of his time to his role as censor as well as to his main function as head of the Royal Household. His principal assistants were the Comptroller of the Office, Sir Terence Nugent, who had held the post since 1936, and the Assistant Comptroller, Sir Norman Gwatkin.[3] Both men were conscientious public servants, but as

1.   Withdrawing a licence from a play in production was a very drastic step even for the Lord Chamberlain's Office, and it happened very rarely. The comedy *Felicity Jasmine* had its licence rescinded in 1944 after it was belatedly realized that the plot turned on a magic potion supposed to cure impotence. In 1948 *A Pin to See the Peepshow*, F. Tennyson Jesse's play based on her own novel about the Thompson-Bywaters case, was refused a licence for the Library Theatre, Manchester, because the brother of the murdered man raised objections. The licence of an earlier play on the same subject, *People Like Us*, by Frank Vosper, written in 1923 but only licensed in 1948, which was already well into its run at Wyndham's Theatre in London, and doing well, was withdrawn by the Lord Chamberlain. The manager Henry Sherek claimed in his autobiography *Not in Front of the Children* that at a meeting in the Office, the Comptroller and his assistant (Nugent and Gwatkin), said to him that if he (Sherek) did not surrender the licence voluntarily, they believed that they had the power to force him to do so. The ban on both plays was only lifted after the death of Mr Thompson's surviving sister in 1964.

2.   Laurence Roger Lumley, 11th Earl of Scarbrough, KG, PC, GCSI (1896–1969). Educated Eton, Sandhurst, and Magdalen College, Oxford. Served in France in 11th Hussars 1916–18. Lord Chamberlain 1952–63.

3.   Lt.-Col. Sir Terence Edmund Gascoigne Nugent GCVO MC, brother of Sir Guy Nugent, 4th Bart.; cr. Lord Nugent 1960. (1895–1973). Educated Eton and

deeply conservative as you would expect men of their age and profession to be. Neither understood modern drama nor pretended to do so; producers who realized this tended to get on with them much better that those who did not.

The plays refused a licence in 1955 were certainly not refused because they were at the unacceptable forefront of modern drama. In June *The Golden Mask*, by Winifred Comstock, was not recommended for licence by its reader Sir St Vincent Troubridge,[4] because one of the characters was deemed to have an unhealthy homosexual relationship. This supposed unwholesomeness is not easy to detect in the script now, but in January 1955 it was enough to have the play turned down flat, and as it was not a particularly good play, nobody felt disposed to fight for its chances. In early November there was one of the earliest appearances in the LCO's records of Paul Raymond, whose nude revues of various kinds still flourish in Soho more than 40 years later. At this stage in his career, he was producing lurid melodramas of crime and prostitution, which in differing guises had been a staple of minor provincial theatres for many years. The play this time was *The Brothel*, by R. Howard Arundel—one wonders how the author or Raymond thought the play was ever going to be licensed with such a title. The reader, Charles Heriot,[5] said of it, 'Neither place of production nor date is given for this piece, and I am afraid that it will become part of the repertoire of the kind of revue that Mr Raymond puts on… A general warning about sadistic exhibitions and erotic displays must also be given…' A day or two later, Gwatkin was writing to the author who had queried the ban, 'The one-act play to which you refer was banned on account of its unrelieved theme of rape, sadism, dirt and murder. Furthermore, the title would not do'. On 18 November Nugent saw Paul Raymond, and in the course of

Sandhurst. Served in Irish Guards in France throughout WW1. Comptroller of the LCO 1936–60, subsequently Lord-in-Waiting to HM the Queen.

Brigadier Sir Norman Wilmshurst Gwatkin GCVO. (1899–1971). Educated Clifton and Sandhurst. Served in Coldstream Guards in 1918. Succeeded Nugent as Comptroller of the LCO in 1960, held office until 1964.

4.   Lt.-Col. Sir Thomas St.Vincent Wallace Troubridge, 5th Bart (1895–1963). Descendant of Nelson's commander-in-chief. Educated Wellington and Sandhurst. Served in King's Royal Rifle Corps throughout WWI; also served with distinction in WWII. Examiner of Plays from 1952. Died in office.

5.   Charles Heriot. Educated at the University of Glasgow; a former actor and producer. Examiner of Plays 1937–68; Senior Examiner from 1958. During the later years of the censorship a lecturer at Morley College.

the interview Raymond asked 'if it would be possible to alter the theme somewhat. I replied that although I didn't wish to discourage him I thought that a very great change would have to be effected in the play before the Lord Chamberlain would consider it. For instance, all the sadistic parts would have to come out and the pornographic parts be very much modified. In fact, the play...would require entirely re-writing. Mr Raymond, strange to say, was quite reasonable and in spite of Mr Hill's somewhat sinister report on him he was very agreeable and appeared quite sensible'.

A more serious dispute over a play had broken out in late October, and the exchanges of epistolary fire were still taking place in November and December. The play was *Zoe*, by Jean Marsan, adapted and translated by Charles Frank. It was, or had been, a successful light comedy in a characteristic French style, and was considered to have a good chance of a decent West End run, although when Donald Albery submitted the script, he must have had some doubts as the entire theme of the play was already said to be fornication and adultery. Troubridge read the play and said in his report, 'It contains no rude words and...I propose to recommend it, but with the warning that it will be placed pretty well at the top of the list of pieces mentioned with horror as having been licensed, when detractors of the Lord Chamberlain are moaning in print about the banning of their favourite plays about sexual perversity'. Scarbrough minuted to Nugent, 'I have read this play & do not feel certain in my mind what course to take. We have no rigid rule about plays in which immorality takes a prominent part—entire plays dealing with unnatural vice—and it is a question of where to draw the line'.

This was indeed the fundamental issue for the Lord Chamberlain's Office not just in the 1950s, but throughout the whole of the twentieth century—where did you draw the line, and, indeed, should you draw a line at all?

The promoters of the play, and the translator and adaptor, Charles Frank, put up a very spirited fight for *Zoe,* and several letters between Frank and the LCO have survived in the file. In a closely-typed three-page letter of 22 November, Frank argued that it was repression, not openness, in the discussion of sexual morality which endangered, as he put it,

> the free enjoyment of a healthy normal sex-life which is stated to be
> essential for the sound development of our youth... I know full well that,
> if *Zoe* will be allowed to be seen and heard, it will make people laugh up

and down the country, and of course there will also be one or two nar-
row-minded voices raised in disapproval. The question is: does that really
matter? What is it in comparison to the good that the play will undoubtedly do? We have all read in the papers and in a number of books that
have recently appeared (*They Stand Apart*, by Judge Tudor Rees and
Harvey J. Usill, and *Homosexuality*, by D.J. West) in what alarming degree
homosexuality is on the increase in this country. I am not surprised...

Frank clearly saw *Zoe* as an encouragement to impressionable young
people *not* to be tempted by unnatural sexual vices, presumably because
the heterosexual activities depicted in *Zoe* were shown to be so much
more fun. However his argument that a play, to which the Lord Chamberlain had refused a licence, was not a danger but really a potential
source of good to the theatre-going public and the world at large, was a
very old one, one that had been regularly used by agents and managers
since the late Edwardian period, when plays about taboo subjects such as
venereal disease and birth control began to be submitted,[6] and the Lord
Chamberlain was not won over. Despite an interview at the LCO, and
another passionate letter from Frank pointing out that *The Little Hut* and
The Little Stranger, translations of plays by André Roussin both licensed
recently, were as daring, if not *more* daring in content than *Zoe,* Gwatkin
finally replied on 9 December, declining to reconsider the issue of a
licence, 'It finally devolves upon him [i.e., the Lord Chamberlain] to
decide where he must draw the line. He cannot subscribe to your con-
tention that free love, promiscuity, or pre-marital relations should be
encouraged as an antidote to possible homosexuality—nor can he agree
with your belief that this play is likely to do a lot of good'.

At the very beginning of 1956, Arthur Miller's *A View from the Bridge*
was sent in by the most powerful of West End managements, H.M.
Tennent, accompanied by a personal letter from Beaumont to Nugent,
'I am enclosing you the script we discussed on the telephone this morning...I am naturally very anxious to have your personal views as to
whether you think the theme would be acceptable'. The letter is signed
'Binkie', and is a good indication of Beaumont's power in the theatre

6.   The most famous example of this genre was probably *Damaged Goods* by
Eugene Brieux, eventually licensed in 1917 after much argument. Note also the
same author's *Maternity*, refused a licence twice, even in a translation by Mrs Bernard
Shaw, before being passed in 1932. There were the avowedly propagandist plays of
Marie Stopes, *Married Love*, *Our Ostriches* and *Vectia* (1923 and 1924), and many
others such as *His Childless Wife* (1918), by Clifford Rean; *Her Unborn Child* (1919),
by F. Barnes; and *Sins of the Parents* (1923), by Aimée Grattan-Clyndes.

world; he had an almost cosy relationship with the LCO, when most managers and promoters scarcely merited the time of day. The play was read by Charles Heriot and recommended for licence—subject to three moderate cuts: the reference to Rodolpho's high voice; the word 'punk', which, Heriot noted, 'is accepted in English as meaning 'a diseased whore'; (perhaps it was in the reign of the first Elizabeth, but by 1956, it was not the immediate meaning that even a well-read theatregoer would have assumed); and, most crucially, the kiss between Eddie and Rodolpho, and the description of it afterwards.

The licence was not actually refused as such, as the play had never been formally submitted, and *A View from the Bridge* was shortly put on under club conditions, at the New Watergate Theatre, where it did very well. To the intense irritation of the LCO, it was advertised as having been 'banned by the censor', something they had gone to a considerable amount of trouble to avoid doing, although what they *had* done had had much the same effect. When eventually the play was licensed, post-Wolfenden Report and the Lord Chamberlain's change of policy,[7] in November 1958, Charles Heriot reported, 'The license for this fine play was left pending until a time and place of production should be assured, and this position was taken advantage of to perform in a club theatre with the proud boast that it had been banned by the censor. This is not so'. Both the LCO and the New Watergate management were being economical with the truth at this point.

Within two weeks' of Binkie Beaumont's initial tactful approach on behalf of Miller's play, another Paul Raymond product, *The Vice Racket,* tersely described by Heriot the examiner as 'another 'vice' one-acter to brighten up a tatty touring revue' was rapidly consigned to the Waiting Box to await details of date and place of performance, and there it remained. It was closely followed by *Hot and Cold in all Rooms,* by Max Reitemann, a light comedy of apparently unexceptionable nature, except that one of the characters was clearly homosexual. The reader was Troubridge who had never been given to tactful circumlocution. He wrote in his report, 'Now as Cecil is a roaring pansy who does not

7.   Since this lecture was delivered in early December 1997, a copy of the memorandum giving details of the new official attitude to homosexual plays finally came to light by chance among the copious papers relating to John Osborne's *A Patriot for Me.* As there have been numerous enquiries as to whether an actual policy document on this subject had been preserved in the Lord Chamberlain's Plays Correspondence, I have transcribed it as an appendix to this article.

pretend to be anything else, and as he is a very central figure, under the present censorship policy as I understand it, the play is not eligible for a licence, and I shall not recommend it'. Despite this apparently blunt rejection, Troubridge was quite sympathetic to the play as a whole, and made several suggestions as to how the character of Cecil could be rendered inoffensive enough for the script to be licensed. Gwatkin minuted,

> It is of course simple to ban a homosexual play or to insist upon the deletion of homosexual passages. Both these courses lay the censorship open to criticism on one side and to credit on the other—such is the inevitable fate of any censorship of art... In the case of this play it is quite unnecessary for the character Cecil to be a homosexual, he could perfectly well be a 'maiden aunt' type of man to whom homosexuality would be just as abhorrent as would normal sex. He hasn't *got* to be a sodomite.

A revised version was submitted in mid-February and Troubridge was able to comment with satisfaction that 'The author has deftly performed the required trick of turning a roaring pansy into a maiden aunt'.

One of the problems of tracing any particular play or theme through the Lord Chamberlain's papers is that not all plays followed a simple path. Most scripts were indeed read, licensed and performed, and their records passed silently into the files, but some, the majority of them touring revues, were passed, disappeared into the provinces on tour, only to spring to unwelcome notice weeks or months later. Such a play was *A Girl Called Sadie*, by 'Eugene Hamilton' (real name David Kirk), recommended for licence by Charles Heriot with all the usual expressions of reluctance. In October the tour had reached Oldham without exciting any undue attention, but there the language and displays of violence provoked a letter from the Oldham police to the LCO to check that what was appearing on stage was in accordance with the licence as issued. No official action was taken at that stage, but the next month the play was on at the Chiswick Empire, where a Mr Gooch of East Sheen saw it and made it the subject of a lengthy letter of complaint to the Lord Chamberlain. The Secretary, R.J. Hill, was deputed to attend a performance and reported

> The piece as allowed contains certain episodes such as a woman practically having a miscarriage on the stage which can only be characterised as disgusting, and others, such as the 'business' of the commencement of sexual intercourse between Albert and Sadie on a couch, which we know from the prosecution in *The Respectable Prostitute*, to offer overwhelming temptation to certain types of actor before certain types of audience.

Doesn't say much for the good people of Oldham or Chiswick, does it? Hill went on,

> I am far from saying, therefore, that in competent hands this play might not be thoroughly undesirable. As it was, however, I am able to report that Jack Gillam [the manager] observed meticulously all the conditions as to dialogue, dress and business laid upon him. And furthermore, that the acting was so inept that the erotic, pathological and tragic climaxes of the play became nothing but bathos leading to laughter all round. Sadie's underclothes which were meant to be daring, were so unsuitable as vehicles for conveying voluptuousness that, given a top-hat, she could have stepped into the circus-ring as the lion-tamer. A not unfunny evening, and no action required.

As soon as the Oldham police had recovered from *A Girl Called Sadie,* than they were confronted by another touring shocker, *Ladies for Hire,* by Dudley Harcourt. This play came with a long history of trouble. As *Lady for Hire,* it had been recommended, wanly, by Troubridge as far back as February 1953. 'It is', he said, 'a poor sensational undesirable play. Only upon removal of the entire flagellation episode is it recommended for licence'. Gwatkin noted on the report on a revised version licensed in 1954, 'This is a vile play and needs no help from us'. Not long after, the appearance of lurid posters for the play's run at the Camberwell Palace—'The play sensation of the year! A startling new sex thriller revealing the naked truth of London's night-life!...ADULTS ONLY'—provoked three local Labour MP's to write to Lord Scarbrough asking him to have the posters removed. He could only reply rather wearily that while he could regulate advertisements on the theatre itself, which he controlled as the *theatre* licensing authority for central London, he had no authority over any other buildings in London, and none over theatre buildings outside central London. In the spring of 1956 he had to inform the Chief Constable of Oldham that he (the Chief Constable) could not operate local rules which ran counter to licensing law, when the Oldham police were proposing to take action against the production there. The play had also interested the police in Southampton, but neither enquiry led to a prosecution. In 1958, the LCO was still regretting that *Ladies for Hire* had ever been licensed, as we shall see.

Back in March 1956, a piece—I hesitate to describe it as a play—called *Halt, Who Goes Bare,* was visited by the Bedford police. In this case, a detective sergeant and woman detective constable attended a performance at the instance of the LCO, to check that the show was being presented in accordance with the licensed script. His Lordship was said to be particularly worried whether the nude poses were exactly the same as those previously licensed, and of which there were, as always, specimen photographs kept on file. Most of the poses for *Halt, Who Goes Bare* had been approved, with one proviso, that the models must not smile. Why a smiling nude should make a pose particularly obscene was not made clear, although perhaps the LCO was harking back to the days when the only kinds of nude display allowed were 'artistic' recreations of famous paintings or statues.

In April another risqué French comedy was submitted, this one called *Pyjama Tops*, a version of *Moumou,* by Jean Letraz, adapted by Mawby Green and E. Feilbert. It was licensed, one of the endorsements being that 'The part of Leonard must not be played as a pansy'. In July the manager, Vincent Shaw, applied to change the title to avoid confusion with *The Pyjama Game*: almost unbelievably he asked to change it to *Bed for Beginners*. This request was rejected, although a change to *The Bed* was allowed. At the end of 1956, the management passed into the hands of Paul Raymond. During the play's run at the Chiswick Empire, there were complaints from members of the public, and R.J. Hill was again sent to watch a performance. A few days later, on 20 December, he sent Raymond a letter severe even by LCO standards.

> There is one feature of the performance, however, to which his Lordship takes the greatest exception, and this is the display made by the three actresses in Act II, when clad in pyjama tops. These tops are made of transparent material., the actresses wear no brassieres underneath, and are in constant, in fact violent movement throughout. The Lord Chamberlain's rules as to actresses moving about the stage with naked breasts are perfectly well known to you...[and could be crudely summarised as 'If it moves, it's rude']... At the Lord Chamberlain's desire I am *once more* [my italics] to tell you that he does not allow actresses to move about the stage with naked breasts, with the breasts visible through transparent coverings, or with merely the nipples covered. In any case nudes, or semi-nudes, even if posed, may not be included in any stage performance within His Lordship's control unless specifically described, and individually allowed by him.

There had also been objections to the copy on the posters displayed outside the theatre. Hill's report of 17 December gave a number of reasons why it was impractical to take any action on this matter. These he had to rehearse again in April 1957 for the Chief Constable of Newport, Monmouthshire, for whom the poster for *The Bed* screaming 'The success lies in the direct and frank attitude to sex and the physical realities of romance... Sets the audience rocking with naughty laughter...even the most daring English vice play is childishly timid compared with this French masterpiece of illicit love...the play that sizzled the censors!' had proved too much.

As I said at the outset, only one play was refused a licence outright in 1956 and that was a pageant called *The Life of Christ*. The reader Geoffrey Dearmer[8] described it as

> a perfectly reverent, dignified and accurate life of Our Lord... Nevertheless the play cannot, of course, be allowed. And quite apart from the law on the subject, it would be grossly unfair to make an exception on account of the play's quite proper and accurate representation, when far better dramatists have necessarily been prevented from attempting it.

The producers of the pageant had been so certain of a licence that they had booked Odsal Stadium, the rugby league ground, and planned a spectacular production with elaborate lighting effects. They had considerable support from the Lord Chamberlain, who added a note to the bottom of the page with Dearmer's report, his pen digging into the paper, with, one presumes, profound irritation.

> Then why are the Mystery Plays in York continually played—under my Presidentship—& to the satisfaction of both Archbishops? Is it because they date originally from the Middle Ages—even though the version now played has been edited & translated in the last few years? Christ is impersonated, and speaks throughout. God Almighty also appears, to say nothing of Satan.

With a distinct and faintly sinister reminiscence of Sir Humphrey Appleby in *Yes Minister*, Gwatkin has pencilled neatly in the margin 'Saw the LC *and explained the matter to him*' (my italics). Almost to the very end of censorship, the ban on the depiction of the Deity on stage remained absolute, and a number of other religious plays were refused a licence in the late 1950s and mid 1960s, usually to the utter astonishment of their authors. The venerable *Green Pastures,* written in 1930, for example, was *never* licensed, though submitted six or seven times, sometimes with support from bishops, and although the play won a Pulitzer Prize, had a long successful run in New York and was made into a film.[9]

8.   Geoffrey Dearmer. A writer, play-reader, and member of the council of the Stage Society. Fought at Gallipoli in WWI. Examiner of Plays 1936–58; Senior Examiner from 1953.

9.   Plays refused a licence between 1956 and 1965 for depicting the Deity: *The*

Ironically, 15 May, the day on which *The Life of Christ* was turned down, was the date supplied for the first performance of Behan's *The Quare Fellow* at the Theatre Royal, Stratford East. It had been licensed with a few minor cuts after a surprisingly sympathetic report by Troubridge. He had not bothered to disguise his own opinions, referring in his usual robust style to the 'fellow travellers of Stratford', and his last paragraph was clearly intended to show how liberal he was. 'I hope justifiably I have allowed this play much latitude over a number of 'bloody's' and lesser oaths. To cut them out would make nonsense of the speech of a lot of low Irish in a play not basically censorable; the language will cause no offence whatsoever in Stratford E...'

A much more typical example of a script nearly turned down, and then licensed, but with major excisions, for the Theatre Royal, Stockport in June, was that for *Les Belle Plume* (sic). The unfortunate writer (and one of the performers) was a small-time producer called Ernie Payne; his show was unsparingly descibed by Heriot as 'a nasty touring revue with a pathological comedian, so-called'. All the material, not just that of the comedian, Derick Arthur, was cut to pieces, and more than half disallowed. Payne's reply of 13 June to the LCO is pathetically misspelt and ill-typed. Speaking of the comedian's script he says (I have attempted to reproduce Payne's grammar and spelling), 'The reason why he sent a good bit up. was for you to sort out a good clean act. which he does. Many thanks for this'. The Lord Chamberlain was required to perform many duties, but acting an unpaid script-doctor to a third-rate touring revue was not one of them. Payne was worried about the part of his script which he claimed had been licensed previously, but he said, rather nervously,

> But to save a lot of worry with the Police. I would like to have it read again in this order... I have had the police to see me each night at Stockport, With this being a new show. and I have Two Licenses with me also the Scripts that has been passed. they are still worring me for the Title... Im going back and forwards to Stockport. with me haveing such a lot to do at my own home etc before I go On tour. When I have had the pic-

Road to Emmaus (1957); *The Boy who Carved Birds* and *The Jesus Revolution* (1961); *Simple Golgotha* and *A Man Dies* (1965). *A Man Dies* was subsequently shown on television and the Lord Chamberlain came in for heavy criticism for his decision to withhold a licence. In 1966, after a House of Lords debate on theatre censorship in which the Bishop of St Albans spoke against the wholesale ban, the Lord Chamberlain, Lord Cobbold, finally ended the prohibition by licensing not only *A Man Dies* but other plays in which the Deity was portrayed.

tures taken of the Two Semi-Nudes I will send these along. But up to now, none of them are poseing semi nude until I get pictures done. I trust you will send me a reply per return, as it will save a lot of trouble. and one cannot work with a lot of worry on their minds. I dont put on a rude show or vulgar show. I never have and dont intend to.

Alas, several of Mr Payne's nude poses *were* disallowed, because the models were smiling in the photographs, and in the first week of the show, the Chief Constable of Cheshire wrote to the LCO for a copy of the script to check that the performers were keeping to the licensed material and poses.

In the second half of the year, homosexual themes and characters in plays became even more of an issue for the Lord Chamberlain. In June a play *The Romantic Age* by Warren Chetham-Strode was submitted for licence. It was read by Charles Heriot, and recommended, with reservations. 'This is by no means a masterpiece, but it does deal with the question of adolescent *schwärmerei* in a sensible, aseptic manner, and makes a good play without unfairly using the material'. A licence was prepared, pending supply of the date and place of production, but as these were never supplied, the licence remains on the file. This contains a revealing memorandum from Gwatkin. 'It would be unhelpful if a justified charge of inconsistency could be proved against the censorship, and I think that we sail very near the wind in this respect regarding some perversion plays. That perversion did not in fact take place, even if this is known by the audience, does not, to my mind, affect the issue; it only makes it slightly worse if it does take place'. In fairness to the benighted Mr Payne of *Les Belle Plume* I should point out here that either Gwatkin or his typist could not spell 'perversion' properly, as the word appears as 'pevertion' throughout the text, despite several efforts to correct the spelling by hand. Gwatkin then lists a large number of plays with homosexual characters and incidents,[10] and ends with 'If we are to have a rule,

10. Gwatkin says at this point 'We say, "we don't pass plays about perversion."' *Serious Charge*. Perversion between man and boy talked about but did not take place—passed.
Now Barabbas. Perversion between men which had taken place—passed.
The Hidden Years. Between schoolboys—passed.
South. Talked about by a man, did not take place—not passed.
Tea and Sympathy. Talked about between man and undergraduate, did not take place —not passed.

it seems that reasonable perversion between boys is passable while perversion between man and man, and man and boy is not. That seems fair as long as we stick to it'. It was very typical of Gwatkin that he did not particularly mind what the rules were, as long as there *were* rules, and they were adhered to.

In September, the Lord Chamberlain licensed a new translation, by the American Dudley Fitts, of the *Lysistrata* of Aristophanes, to be produced at the Oxford Playhouse and then to go on tour. Troubridge had conscientiously if ponderously considered the potential embarrassment for the Lord Chamberlain in 'banning a work that has been an acknowledged comic masterpiece since the year 411 B.C. He appended a long list of risqué lines to be considered for amendment or excision, quoted (with approval) Gilbert Murray complaining of a new translation done for the Cambridge Theatre back in 1931,[11] and finally declined to recommend a licence. He was decisively overruled by Scarbrough, who wrote at the bottom of the report, 'I cannot overlook the fact that seven versions have been passed since 1910 (2 others banned) and that this translation appears to be a scholarly effort... It would need to be particularly outrageous to deserve banning & I do not think that drastic course is necessary', and authorized the issue of a licence subject to some minor cuts in dialogue and a general warning about indecency of action. In a reversal of the normal course of events, whereby a touring play only attracted complaints when it left the sophisticated metropolis for the more strait-laced towns and cities of the North and Midlands, this *Lysistrata* toured quietly until it reached the Duke of York's Theatre in London in late 1957. Not only were there letters of complaint to the LCO at this point ('This play is rotten with obscenity!'), but one night in March 1958 there was also a full-scale public disturbance at the theatre. Leaflets were flung from the gallery reading, 'AN APPEAL TO THE BRITISH PUBLIC. WRITE TO YOUR M.P. AND DEMAND THAT THE LORD CHAMBERLAIN IN FUTURE REFUSES LICENCE TO

The Children's Hour. Females—not passed.
A View from the Bridge. Man vaguely accused of being abnormal—not passed.
Third Party. Originally obviously perversion between two men during the war; we tried to turn it into ordinary friendship and passed it.
The Golden Mask. Entirely about perversion—not passed.
The Romantic Age. Between schoolboys—not passed?'
    11. Murray in a letter to Granville Barker 'Under modern conditions it is merely an exercise in obscenity. Damn them!' This translation was one of the two versions of the *Lysistrata* banned.

DISGUSTING PLAYS LIKE THIS'. As a result of this outburst, both producers were abruptly summoned to the LCO for a severe dressing-down. Poor Lord Scarbrough was even attacked for having licensed, not an obscene play, but a poor translation: a Miss Beatrice Dawson wrote to him describing Pitts' text as 'this suburban & quite revolting distortion of Aristophanes' play'. The Lord Chamberlain replied to her with measured politeness that he could not judge the translation as he could not read ancient Greek.

July saw the unwelcome recrudescence of a touring revue *Wonderful Time* which had been licensed in its original form in 1952, most of the papers on the file relating to complaints in that year about the supposed obscenity of the material used by the comedian, Ted Ray. By the time the revue attracted attention again in 1956, the issue was whether the production was a stage play, in part or in whole—in which case the *entire* script had to be licensed—or a variety show, in which case the Lord Chamberlain's licence was not required and the performance came under local licensing regulations. At the Empire Theatre, Newcastle-on-Tyne, the one slight dramatic sketch that had caused the whole of the script to come under the Lord Chamberlain's notice was taken out of the running order to allow the entertainment to proceed as a variety show, but it was then discovered that the *theatre* did not have the correct licence for music and dancing. The LCO cut the Gordian knot by declaring that *Wonderful Time* in fact *was* a stage play which needed a licence, and the promoter Val Parnell found himself writing a very contrite letter promising that he would not try the same manoeuvre again.

The LCO faced much the same problem with a Paul Raymond revue entitled *Les nues de Paris*, submitted in late July. Having initialled Heriot's grudging recommendation for licence, Lord Scarbrough angrily scribbled out his 'S' and added testily 'I object to giving this a licence. It seems to me a farce to pretend that this is a stage play. What would be the implications of refusing a licence?' In a memorandum of 3 August, Gwatkin listed the insuperable difficulties involved in this course of action, and Scarbrough had to agree that a licence could issue. His only victory was to insist that the title be changed to 'something less prurient', which it was, becoming *Le cirque de Paris* instead.

In late October the Robert Anderson play *Tea and Sympathy* came before the Lord Chamberlain for the third time. In November 1953, Binkie Beaumont had used the same 'softly-softly' approach which he was to try again with *A View from the Bridge* in January 1956. On this earlier occasion he got a rather more abrupt reply from Nugent, 'I return herewith the script... We both (i.e. Nugent and Gwatkin) came independently to the same conclusion—namely that it would be a waste of your time to submit this play for licence...' Donald Albery tried again with a formal submission in 1954, without success. In 1955, Mrs Frank who owned the rights to the play even offered to fly the Lord Chamberlain and his staff out to Chicago where the play was enjoying a successful run with Deborah Kerr in the role of the schoolmaster's wife, in the hope that this would soften his attitude. The reason for Beaumont and Albery trying once more in 1956 was that they knew that a film of the play, based on the successful Chicago production and with Deborah Kerr again in the lead role, was in the offing, and they wanted to get in first.

They requested a meeting at the Lord Chamberlain's Office, and in mid-October came to see Sir Norman Gwatkin, a meeting minuted in detail by him later the same day. After some skirmishing on the subject of censorship in general, and plays dealing with homosexual themes in particular, Gwatkin had pointed out that

> the Lord Chamberlain took a great deal of trouble to gauge the general feeling about the licensing of such plays and that the feeling was against such action. They [Beaumont and Albery] suggested, nicely, that the sort of people the Lord Chamberlain asked were as likely to agree to licensing such plays as the House of Lords were to agree to the nationalisation of land...

At the end of the month, Lord Scarbrough, Nugent, and Gwatkin all attended a private showing of the film of *Tea and Sympathy* which Gwatkin later described in a note on the file as 'a very tedious 2 hours', although a hand in the margin, possibly Lord Scarbrough's, has added 'not for me'. All homosexual references had been excised from the film —Beaumont and Albery had claimed to Gwatkin at their earlier meeting that they had not—but the Lord Chamberlain would still not modify his stance. When Gwatkin spoke to Albery on 31 October about a number of proposals aired in their previous long discussion on 25 October, no sort of compromise was on offer. In particular, Albery's suggestion that he and Beaumont might open another venue as a theatre club in order to stage *Tea and Sympathy*, because *A View from the Bridge* was still doing so well at their existing club venue, the New Watergate, was greeted with a veiled threat. Gwatkin said that if Albery went ahead with the plan, 'the Lord Chamberlain would feel obliged to reconsider the position of such theatres'; in other words, the LCO would cease to turn a convenient blind eye to the activities of theatre clubs, and subject them to all the conditions of the Theatres Act.

It was another two years before *Tea and Sympathy* finally received a licence: it was submitted on the same day in November 1958, following the Lord Chamberlain's change of policy on homosexual plays, as *A View from the Bridge* and *Cat on a Hot Tin Roof*. The five years since its original submission had not done the play any favours and Heriot, in recommending it for licence said plainly, 'This is the earliest of the plays to be submitted after the recent change of policy. It is a pity that it isn't a better play'. Quality notwithstanding, the Lord Chamberlain's Office was still receiving complaints from the public about *Tea and Sympathy* in 1960.

Finally, a glimpse of what awaited the Lord Chamberlain and his staff in 1957. Before January was out, they had to deal with what was quite possibly one of the worst plays ever submitted for licence, The author was an elderly theatre critic and melodramatist called Walter Saltoun, who had first submitted a play for licence (*A Man and his Money*) in 1910. That he had no conception, even after 40 years of playwriting, of what the Lord Chamberlain could be expected to license, can be gauged by the title of his 1957 effort—*Sex*. The script was read by Charles Heriot, who gamely listed some of Saltoun's previous dramas, beginning with *The Abode of Love*.[12] 'Since then', he continued grimly, 'he has been getting older and dirtier. The present offering is a stilted piece of pure pornography'. After recounting a plot crammed with sordid incident which would have made Paul Raymond blush with embarrassment, if not with shame, Heriot concludes his summary, 'As if this was not enough, Tony [the villain], on the way to prison, has a vision of his saintly father, a parson, who calls on him to repent. Tony drinks cyanide, and with this speech 'Too late, my friend! Give this, my dying speech, to the world. Crime does not pay. The cost is too high' dies. This nauseating mixture of sex, sadism, coprology, and sentiment is *not recommended* for licence'. His judgment was echoed by Gwatkin who noted, 'Yes. Rarely have I read such schoolboy dirt'. Saltoun fired off three

12. Saltoun's plays, several written in collaboration with Aimée Grattan-Clyndes, included: *The Abode of Love* (refused 1912, passed 1915); *What Women Will Do for Love* (1915); *Her Forbidden Sacrifice* and *Her Day of Reckoning* (1916); *The Man She Bought,* and *A Married Man's Sweetheart* (1918); *Married Sinners* and *A Bad Woman* (also known as *What Is Home without a Mother?* and *The Curse of Marriage*) (1919).

long letters to the Lord Chamberlain before the end of February, his last complaining that *Sex* was far less violent than *Ladies for Hire*—another vice-melodrama which had plagued the LCO since its original licence had been granted in 1953. Despite a third, and somewhat frigid letter of rejection from Sir Norman, Saltoun was not prepared to give up hope for his play. After the change in policy on plays with homosexual themes, Saltoun wrote once more asking whether the new policy would mean that *Sex* could at last be passed. *Sex* was never passed, and the Lord Chamberlain's reply to this letter has not been preserved in the files.

Look Back in Anger, licensed at the end of January 1956 with some modest amendments, did not change the world for the Lord Chamberlain. He was still more likely to be worrying about the licence for *My Fair Lady,* where Sir St Vincent Troubridge was earnestly considering in his report whether the famous 'Not bloody likely' of *Pygmalion* could be amended to 'Move your blooming arse!' to preserve its shock value in the third quarter of the twentieth century. For Lord Scarbrough, Sir Terence, Sir Norman, R.J. Hill, the Secretary, and Charles Heriot and the other examiners, controlling English drama was a continuous process, a matter of 'holding the line', or even trying to draw it afresh, for the line, whatever the Lord Chamberlain's Office decided, was always moving.

APPENDIX

Transcripts of Lord Chamberlain's memorandum on change of policy on homo-sexual plays, dated 31 October 1958.

I have decided to make a change in the policy of the censorship, and I think it desirable to place on record as clearly as possible the nature of the change so that all concerned may be fully aware of it.

First, the reason behind this change. For some time the subject of homosexuality has been so widely debated, written about and talked about, that it is no longer justifiable to continue the strict exclusion of this subject from the stage. I do not regret the policy of strict exclusion which has been continued up to now, and I think it has been to the public good. Nevertheless, now that it has become a topic of almost everyday conversation, its exclusion from the stage can no longer be defended as a reasonable course, even when account is taken of the more effective persuasion which the living stage can exercise as compared with the written word. I therefore propose to allow plays which make serious and sincere attempt to deal with the subject. It will follow also that references also in other plays will be allowed to the subject which appear necessary to the dialogue or to the plot, and which are not salacious or offensive. *Licences will continue to be refused for plays which are exploitations of the subject* rather than contributions to the problem; and similarly refer-ences to the subject which are unnecessary or have merely an exploitation value will be disallowed.

I do not imagine that this change of policy will eliminate all difficulties with regard to this question. I have, in fact, little doubt that we shall continue to be faced with problems which it will be difficult to resolve. It may, however, help the Examiners of Plays if I answer a few questions which are likely to arise:-

(a)   Every play will continue to be judged on its merits. The difference will be that plays will be passed which deal seriously with the subject.

(b)   We would not pass a play that was violently pro-homosexual.

(c)   We would not allow a homosexual character to be included if there were no need for such inclusion.

(d)   We would not allow any 'funny' innuendoes or jokes on the sub-ject.

(e)   We will allow the word 'pansy', but not the word 'bugger'.

(f)   *We will not allow embraces between males or practical demonstrations of love.*

(g)   We will allow criticism of the present homosexual laws, though plays obviously written for propaganda purposes will fail to be judged on their merits.

(h)   We will not allow embarrassing display by male prostitutes.

REFERENCES FOR PLAYS CITED IN TEXT

'List 1' and 'List 2' refer to the lists of unlicensed plays, the former being those refused a licence, the latter those 'not submitted in accordance with the Theatres Act', usually known as 'Waiting Box' plays. For full details of Lord Chamberlain's Plays Collections shelfmarks, and how to order material, please see the Department's leaflets on the play collections.

★ indicates a play for which full and accurate references were not available at time of writing, because of the ongoing transfer of the play collections and the indexes to the new British Library at St Pancras.

	Script	File
Look Back in Anger	1956/15	56/8932
The Life of Christ	List 1/33	LR 1956
The Golden Mask	List 1/33	LR 1955
The Brothel	List 1/33	LR 1955
Zoe	List 1/33	LR 1955
The Little Hut ★	1950	
	1953	53/5858
The Little Stranger ★	1954	54/6694
A View from the Bridge	1958/51	58/1463
The Vice Racket	List 2/22	WB 1956
Hot and Cold in all Rooms	1956/11	56/8872
A Girl Called Sadie	1956/13	56/8903
The Respectable Prostitute	1947/9	47/7906
	1958/21	58/995
Ladies for Hire	1953/4	53/5030
Halt, Who Goes Bare	1956/19	56/9009
Pyjama Tops (later The Bed)	1956/23	56/9088
Green Pastures ★	1930	LR 1930
The Quare Fellow	1956/27	56/9158
Les Belle Plume	1956/32	56/9243
The Romantic Age	List 2/22	WB 1956
Lysistrata	1956/41	56/9372
Wonderful Time	1956/37	56/9320
Les Nues de Paris (later Le Cirque...)	1956/38	56/9329
Tea and Sympathy	1958/50	58/1459
Cat on a Hot Tin Roof ★	List 2/21	
	1964/43	64/4496
A Man and his Money	1910/7	10/410
Sex	List 1/34	LR 1957

	Script	File
The Abode of Love	1915/19	15/3599
My Fair Lady ★	1956	
Felicity Jasmine	List 1/29	LR 1944
A Pin to See the Peepshow ★	List 1/30	LR 1948
	1964	
People Like Us ★	1964	
Damaged Goods	List 1/4	
	1917/6	17/837
Maternity	List 1/5	LR 1918
	List 1/8	LR 1924
	1932/28	32/11570
Married Love	List 1/7	LR 1923
Our Ostriches	List 1/7	LR 1923
	1923/27	23/5104
	1930/23	30/9705
Vectia	List 1/8	LR 1924
His Childless Wife	List 1/5	LR 1918
Her Unborn Child	List 1/6	LR 1919
Sins of the Parents	List 1/7	LR 1923
The Road to Emmaus	List 1/34	LR 1957
The Boy who Carved Birds	List 1/35	LR 1961
The Jesus Revolution	List 1/35	LR 1962
Simple Golgotha ★		LR 1965
A Man Dies	1966/23	66/883
Serious Charge	1953/21	53/5355
Now Barabbas	1947/7	47/7860
The Hidden Years ★	1947	
South	1959/12	59/1791
The Children's Hour	1964/40	64/4458
The Abode of Love	1915/19	15/3599
What Women Will Do for Love	1912/25	12/637
Her Forbidden Sacrifice	1916/20	16/420
Her Day of Reckoning	1916/34	16/714
The Man She Bought ★	1918	
A Married Man's Sweetheart	1918/15	18/1755
Married Sinners	1919/25	19/2555
A Bad Woman	1919/18	19/2349

INDEXES

INDEX OF PLAYS CITED

INDEX OF PEOPLE